STAND UP for YOUR RIGHTS

Editors:

Paul Atgwa, Kenya
Jasper Bakyayita, Uganda
Damien Boltauzer, Canada
Gözde Boga, Turkey
Alberto Granada, Colombia
Vivek Guha, India
Christine Jasinski, Belgium
Alejandro Jiménez Cabal, Mexico
Sheku Syl Kamara, Sierra Leone
Bremley W. B. Lyngdoh, India
Sayed Mosediq, Afghanistan
Daniel Juwel Ngungoh, Cameroon
Toyin Ajasa-Oluwa, UK
Joseph Robert, France
Leah Thigpen, USA
Lissa Wheen, UK
Alexander Woollcombe, UK
Jeta Xharra, Kosovo, Yugoslavia

ⓖ

Design and illustration team:

Riffat Lotia, Pakistan
Jantien Roozenburg, The Netherlands
Arshak Sarkissian, Armenia
Urjana Shrestha, Nepal
Sanid Zuko, Bosnia-Herzegovina

We would like to thank the following for their generous support of this project:
The Ministry of Foreign Affairs of The Netherlands;
The MacArthur Foundation; The Samuel Rubin Foundation;
The Reuters Foundation; The Polden-Puckham Charitable Foundation;
The Body Shop Foundation; The Armenian General Benevolent Union;
The Positive Spirit Network

Thanks also to Amnesty International, Anti-Slavery International, Children of the Andes, Gerison Lansdown, Margot Brown, Tina Jorgensen, Tom Jolly, Dan Jones, Rupert Woollcombe, Eirwen Harbottle, and Richard Wheen for their help and advice, to the Bob Marley Foundation for allowing us to include lyrics from the song "Get Up, Stand Up," and IPM, as exclusive licensor of the King Estate, for the Martin Luther King, Jr., quote.

Peace Child International
Project co-ordinator: Rosey Simonds
Youth project co-ordinator: Esther Vivas Esteve
Designer: Julian Olivier
Editorial adviser: David Woollcombe

Two-Can Publishing
Editorial Director: Jane Wilsher
Art Director: Belinda Webster
Production Director: Lorraine Estelle
Editorial support: Lucy Arnold, Leila Peerun

First published in the United States by
World Book, Inc.
525 West Monroe Street
Chicago, Illinois 60661

For information on other World Book Products, call 1-800-255-1750 x2238, or visit our Website at http://www.worldbook.com

© 1998 Peace Child International
The White House, Buntingford, Herts SG9 9AH, UK
British Registered Charity No. 284731

Hardback ISBN 0-7166-0352-7
Paperback ISBN 0-7166-0353-5
Library of Congress Catalog Card Number 98-61244

Printed in the United States of America

Photographic credits
p4 Supplied by the UN High Commission for Refugees; p14 Supplied by the UN; p27 Both supplied by Anti-Slavery International; p31 Supplied by the South African High Commission for Refugees; p34 Supplied by Amnesty International; p40 Photo by Visar Krueziu; p48 Supplied by Amnesty International; p50 Supplied by Michael Aris; p84 Photo of Kosovo demonstration by Visar Krueziu.
All other photographs were taken by the young contributors.

Front cover illustration: Helen D'Souza
Illustrations for Article headings: Urjana Shrestha, 18, Nepal
Map p6-7: Mel Pickering

Publisher's note

This book represents a year's work by the young members of the Peace Child International network. They gathered facts, interviews, opinions, stories, poems, and photographs from young people all around the world. This material was then pulled together by a group of young editors to provide fresh perspectives and a commentary on the Universal Declaration of Human Rights.

Each Article of the Declaration is considered, but some Articles are dealt with in more detail than others. The editors ask questions about the issues and highlight aspects with original material from the young contributors, along with their own editorial comment. The book reflects their own ideas and opinions based on their personal experiences, but final decisions on what was included in the book were made by the publishers.

The writing is often intensely personal. However, this thought-provoking material makes an excellent starting point for discussions about human rights both in and out of the classroom. The final pages are filled with opportunities for action and contacts for organizations involved in trying to fight for a free and fair world. The last sections of the book are useful for teachers and students, particularly pages 80-81.

The publishers made every effort to verify the facts, but not all information could be substantiated, especially that given in personal accounts. The views and opinions of the contributors are not necessarily those of the publishers, the United Nations, or any other organization mentioned.

"Human Chain" by Srijana Shrestha, 15, Nepal

Contents

Foreword

by Mary Robinson, United Nations High Commissioner for Human Rights

"The objective of all human rights action is simply this: to ensure a life of dignity for each person on this earth. The question is, how? What makes sense to people who live a comfortable, secure life may make no sense at all to those living on the margins of society. This is a problem I am aware of every day in my job. I find that two words help me a lot in dealing with this problem: respect—*really listening and hearing each side's point of view—and* responsibility—*finding the balance between securing my own rights and learning to live by them responsibly so that someone else is not deprived of his or her rights.*

Another word I use often is together. *I believe the old Native American saying: The hurt of one is the hurt of all. A single abused child is a scar on the face of the global family. Our lives will not be completely dignified until we all can achieve a basic level of dignity.*

This is a difficult task. Your generation faces the most daunting challenges as we move into the new millennium: abuse of children, environmental destruction, civil wars, corruption, inequality, nuclear proliferation. I believe we can tackle all of these only if we build our society on a solid foundation of human rights. Our approach must be directed by the principles that you will read about in these pages—the principles of the Universal Declaration of Human Rights— which are as relevant today as when they were adopted in 1948.

Human rights work never stops. Many laws and treaties have been passed, but they need to be implemented. We must always be vigilant. Fifty years ago, children did not talk much about human rights—in fact, most people did not talk about them in the way we do today. Now, thanks to the work done since then and to television and the Internet, we can know immediately when someone's rights are being abused, even if it is far away. Yet abuses continue, which is why this project is important. You are starting now on the road to defend your rights and the rights of others around the world.

I congratulate the young authors and editors of this book for their dedication in educating themselves about human rights. You will read some distressing stories here, but you will also read of heroism. Yes, we have come a long way since the Declaration was signed—apartheid and colonialism have almost disappeared and more people are expressing themselves freely than at any other time in history. You should celebrate the achievements, while acknowledging how far we still have to go. You are taking the first step by picking up this book. Learning about human rights is essential, but you must remember the steps that follow: to live by a philosophy of human rights and to work to secure them for everyone."

Mary Robinson

A message **from the editors**

Hi friends—

We're so happy that you are sitting down to read our book because we, the editors, have had such a good time editing and designing it. Thousands of young people from all over the world helped us make it. We hope it reflects the ideas and dreams of each and every one. We should explain how this book came about. Back in 1993, several young people got together over lunch at a UN Human

Finalizing the text was not always easy. Even within our own group, there were different opinions about what human rights are. This made the experience something extraordinary. But we respected our differences, and we agreed on one thing—everyone should have equal human rights.

Rights Conference in Vienna, Austria. They thought it would be a good idea for young people everywhere to write about human rights. In 1997, they sent thousands of requests to schools and youth groups worldwide, asking for poems, reports, and pictures about human rights. In April 1998, 11 young editors from nine countries sorted the material. They put together a first draft of the book, which was sent to contributors for their comments. It was also sent to a team of human rights educators and experts for review and guidance. Then, in July 1998, we—the lucky ones chosen to be the final editors—arrived in England at the headquarters of Peace Child International. We reviewed all the material and got it ready to go to the printer.

We hope you enjoy the result of our efforts. Working on this book has made us really positive about making our world a better place.

The editors

Thanks to **everybody**

We would like to say a big thank you to all the people who sent in material for this book. As you can see from this map, the contributors come from all over the planet. There were so many different stories, pictures, and case studies that it was impossible to include them all. We tried our best to make sure that we included a wide variety of ideas from different parts of the world.

Listed below are the names of groups and individuals that took part in *Stand Up for Your Rights.*

AFGHANISTAN
NATURE

ALGERIA
Peace Child International – Algeria

ARGENTINA
Andrés López
Asociación para el Progreso de la Educación,
Escuela No. 12 Cornelio Saavedra
Escuela No. 23 Almafuerte
Escuela No. 34 Dra. Carolina Tobar Garciá,
Escuela No. 37 Bernardino Rivadavia
Escuela No. 66 SES Quincentenario de la
    Independencia Argentina
Escuela San Patricio
Instituto de Secundaria Saúl Taborda
Misión Rescate-Argentina
Pamela Castro
Team Work
Valeria Gilardone

AUSTRALIA
Oz Child

BENIN
Mission Terre-Benin

BOSNIA-HERZEGOVINA
First Bosniak High School
Saburina Primary School

BURKINA FASO
Association de Protection et de Sauvegarde de
    l'Enfance en Danger

CAMEROON
Environmental Club
Rescue Mission-Cameroon

CANADA
Spruce Glen Public School
Whycocomagh Consolidated School

COMOROS
Sitti Fatouma Ahmed

COSTA RICA
Casa Alianza-Regional Office
Centro Educativo Campestre

CYPRUS
CYN English School
CYN Magosa Sub-Group

CZECH REPUBLIC
Slavonic High School
UNESCO Club Olomouc

DEMOCRATIC REPUBLIC OF THE CONGO
Collège AH 12 Septembre

FINLAND
Ethics 5-6 Roihuvuori Primary School
Puolalanmäki Agenda 21 Group

FRANCE
CM2 Ronchece
Collège Blaise Pascal

GAMBIA
Baroteh Primary School
Kotu Senior Secondary School
Rescue Mission Sub-Group Advocating for Human
    Rights

GEORGIA
School No.122

GERMANY
UNESCO Projekt Schule

GHANA
Accra Academy
Accra High School
Deks Junior Secondary School
Eco Club of the Earth
Rescue Mission-Ghana

INDIA
Bhima Sangha
Child Association to Renascence to Earth (CARE)
Concerned for Working Children
Consortium of Indian Scientists for Sustainable
    Development
Free The Children-India
Maharaja Sawai Man Singh Vidyalaya
Mahila Akta Samiti & Srijan

INDONESIA
KKSP Foundation

KENYA
Environmental Club
Environmental Protection and Community
    Development
KURM
Wamba Secondary School

LITHUANIA
Silainiai Secondary School

MACEDONIA
First Children's Embassy in the World

MEXICO
Misión Rescate-Mexico

SPAIN
Collegi Sant Andreu
Defensa de los Niños Internacional
Elena Noguera i Pigem
Escola Joan Pelegrí

SRI LANKA
Interactive Media Group

SWEDEN
Bagarmossens Skola 3A

SWITZERLAND
Collège du Léman
International School Geneva

TOGO
Club Ecolo-Pacifiste

TURKEY
Turkey Mission
Turkish Club of Human Rights

UGANDA
African Network for Prevention and
    Protection Against Child Abuse and
    Neglect
Children's Advocates
Naddangira Mixed Child Rights Club
Nsangi Primary School
Rescue Mission-Uganda
St. John Bosco Katende Primary School

UNITED KINGDOM
Fallibroome High School
Fulford Amnesty Group
George Mitchell School
King Manor School
Mill Mead School
Newminster Middle School
Saint Mary's School
Trinity Junior School
Ward Freeman School

UNITED STATES OF AMERICA
Beasley Academic Center
Decatur Classical School
Evergreen Academy
Garrett A. Morgan Elementary School
Girls Inc.
Ira F. Aldridge Elementary School
Kenwood High School
Lane Technical High School
Lenart School
Maria Saucedo Scholastic Academy
Nash School
Newberry Academy
Ray School
Robert Heahs Elementary
Vanderpoel School

YUGOSLAVIA
Postpessimists
United Games

NEPAL
Kathmandu Group
Peace Child Nepal

THE NETHERLANDS
Gymnasium Haganum

NIGERIA
Child Rights Club
Ebonite Foundation
Nigeria Society for the Improvement of Rural
    People
YIELD

PAKISTAN
ABSA
Al-Madrassa-tul-Saifiya-tul Burhania
Bay View High School
Beaconhouse Public School
C.A.S. School
City School
Foundation Public School
Habib Girls' School
Happy Home School
Human Rights Education Programme
Nasra Secondary School
Pakistan Environmental Lobbying Society
St. Joseph's Convent School

PALESTINE
Greenpeace Palestine

PERU
Asociación ECOBOY
Asociación Pukllasunchis
Centro de Investigación y Desarrollo de la
    Educación
Colegio Jose Antonio Encinas
Grupo SAYWITE
Lima Young Persons Agenda 21 (LYPA 21)
L@s niñ@s y jovenes de San Francisco
Misión Rescate-Peru
Tierra Viva

PHILIPPINES
Badian National High School
Children and Peace Philippines
Samahan ng mga Anak ng Desaparecidos,

RUSSIA
Physico-Technical Lyceum #1

SENEGAL
Défense des Enfants International Section 1
Ecole de Formation G. Legoff

SOUTH AFRICA
Realitivity
Rescue Mission Gimmies

SOUTH KOREA
Sarangbang Group for Human Rights

Get up, stand up... read on

Do you know what your rights are? Did you know that more than 170 governments have made an agreement that everyone has the right to life, that you can't lock up people without a proper trial, and that you are free to practice whatever religion you want? In 1948, the members of the UN General Assembly came together in Paris and agreed to the "Universal Declaration of Human Rights." This document sets out the rights to which everyone is entitled.

This book celebrates the Declaration. In its 30 Articles, the document defines the meaning and value of life. It is not just for people living in faraway places, in war zones, or under oppressive dictatorships. It is about us, and about the way we live our lives! Many feel it is the most important document the United Nations has ever produced.

As we started to work on this book, we realized that the issue of human rights is complicated. For example, many people think that human rights are a luxury of prosperous countries. Other people question which is more important—a country that observes human rights laws or one whose people have jobs, homes, and enough to eat? Still other people feel that nongovernmental organizations (NGO's) and the United Nations act like a human rights police force that is ignorant of the causes of problems and throws out traditions that have served for thousands of years.

Then there is the question of how human rights should be enforced. Recently, there was an agreement to set up an international criminal court to punish leaders of countries who abuse the human rights of their citizens. But in the past, the power of such courts has proved limited.

We who worked on this book decided that the most straightforward and effective way of thinking about and enforcing human rights is to believe in them and teach them, to live by them every day, and to stand up for them if need be.

We soon began to wonder what to call this book. There were plenty of ideas, but in the end we went for *Stand Up for Your Rights* from the famous song "Get Up, Stand Up" by Bob Marley. Here are just a few lines from the song:

Illustration by Jantien Roozenburg, 15, The Netherlands

*Most people think great God will come
from the sky,
Take away ev'rything, and make
ev'rybody feel high,
But if you know what life is worth,
You would look for yours on earth.
And now you see the light,
You stand up for your right, yeah!*

*So you'd better get up, stand up,
Stand up for your right.
Get up, stand up,
Don't give up the fight.*

How this book is organized

In this book we've divided the Declaration into two broad sections and explored each of its 30 Articles in turn. The Articles in Part One deal with legal and political issues, such as freedom and equality for all people. Part Two addresses themes relating to the day-to-day quality of life of an individual. Each Article is written in plain language at the top of the page. You can find the original wording of each Article at the back of the book, on pages 90-91. Also at the back of the book, in plain language, is the Convention on the Rights of the Child, pages 92-93. This document looks at human rights issues that particularly concern children.

Wherever possible we have credited articles and illustrations to the contributor and given his or her age, but unfortunately we did not always have this information.

You will find several different kinds of type on these pages:
1. **The introduction for each Article and spread is written in bold-faced type.**
2. Passages reported by us in the third person are in plain type.
3. **"** *Other passages, written in italics and contained within quotation marks, are direct accounts in the first person.* **"**
4. *Fictional stories and poems are given in italics without quotation marks.*

You can look up difficult words in our glossary at the end of the book, on pages 94-95.

At the back of the book, you can also find out about groups that have challenged abuses of human rights and changed the world forever. You'll also learn details of how to get involved. It's time to change our world and make it a much better place. It's up to us to make it happen—NOW!

Our dreams...

We allowed ourselves to dream of a world in the future where all human rights are observed. Each of our dreams was different, but there were certain common themes. Dreams are essential if we want to build a better world. By dreaming, we figure out what we really want. These dreams can become our ideal and change the way we lead our lives.

Martin Luther King, Jr. (1929-1968), dreamed of a society where everyone was equal. In 1963, he delivered his stirring "I Have a Dream" speech, which defined the moral basis of the civil rights movement in the United States during the 1950's and 1960's. The poem below is based on that speech. (To find out more about King, turn to page 30.)

*I have a dream
to fight for the rights of the people
I have a dream
to make our environment clean and
green
I have a dream
of good education for children
I have a dream
to fly free as a bird.*

*I have a dream
to make friends of every race
I have a dream
to get peace in the world
I have a dream
not to have war anywhere
I have a dream
to eliminate world poverty.*

*I have a dream
I have lots of dreams...
I want every dream to come true –
But how?
Let's march forward hand in hand
and shoulder to shoulder
To make everyone's dream
come true!!!*

The quest for human rights has a long history, which is often dominated by the abuse of rights, rather than by observance. Turn to the next page and travel with us down the road that led to the Universal Declaration in 1948, and then see what has happened since.

Illustration by Urjana Shrestha, 18, Nepal

The **highs** and **lows** of human rights

The Magna Carta, signed in England in 1215, was the first attempt by a people to limit the divine right of kings. The U.S. Bill of Rights, which describes the fundamental liberties of the people in the United States, took effect in 1791.

An early example of rules of human conduct is the Ten Commandments, believed to have been given to Moses by God.

The ancient Greeks told the story of Antigone. She has come to symbolize courage against unjust use of power by a government.

In some cultures, religion provided an excuse for abusing human rights. Inquisitions, human sacrifice, and other cruel rituals were practiced.

Colonial expansion: Beginning in the 1400's, powerful European nations created empires in Africa, Asia, Latin America, and Oceania. As a result, many people in the colonized lands lost what we now think of as human rights.

Slavery: Certainly one of the worst abuses of human rights was the purchase of people as slaves. From the 1400's, Africans were transported in appalling conditions to work in the Americas. Many died as a result.

End of empires: In the 1800's, Simon Bolivar led South America to independence. Gandhi helped India gain independence in 1947. And by the early 1960's, most of the rest of the world was decolonized.

The release of Nelson Mandela from prison in 1990 marked the beginning of the end of apartheid in South Africa.

The Universal Declaration of Human Rights was signed by the United Nations in 1948. It was drawn up by an international committee chaired by former First Lady Eleanor Roosevelt.

Karl Marx hoped communism would give power and rights to the working class. In practice it often gave power to dictators like Stalin, who ruled the former USSR throughout the 1930's and 1940's.

The symbolic barrier to human rights in Eastern Europe, the Berlin Wall in Germany, began to be taken down in November 1989. The end of communism brought greater freedom, but also new challenges to millions.

Illustration by Michael Troukades, 17, Cyprus

When human cultural development began to accelerate rapidly about 35,000 years ago, it's possible that there soon came to be concern about what we now call "human rights."

Some ancient kings and tribal leaders had enormous power. Sometimes they ignored the human rights of the people they ruled when they used their great power.

French Revolution: A great revolt against the divine right of kings was spurred in 1789 when the French National Assembly adopted the Declaration of the Rights of Man and of the Citizen.

In 1839, two men who had been enslaved began a rebellion on a transport ship called *La Amistad*. They were arrested when the ship reached New York. In 1841, the U.S. Supreme Court decided that the rebels were free people who were justified in rebelling.

American Revolution: The American Colonies started fighting a war against British rule in 1775. On July 4, 1776, they declared independence!

UNIVERSAL EDUCATION

Universal education: During the 1800's, many very young children were sent to work instead of school until the benefits of a well-educated work force were acknowledged.

The American Civil War was fought from 1861 to 1865 over the issue of slavery.

WHITES ONLY

Women in Canada won the right to vote in 1918. The 19th Amendment to the U.S. Constitution was ratified in 1920, giving U.S. women the right to vote.

Apartheid and segregation: Slavery was replaced by a new and insidious way of judging people by the color of their skin. From 1948 to 1991 in South Africa, a system known as apartheid rigidly segregated people according to race.

Eleanor Roosevelt and how the Universal Declaration was signed

Over 50 years ago, Eleanor Roosevelt (1884-1962), widow of President Franklin D. Roosevelt (1882-1945), was elected chair of the United Nations Human Rights Commission that wrote the Universal Declaration. She and her colleagues tried to define what is really meant by "human rights." The fact they agreed at all, and at a speed amazing to modern diplomats, was largely due to the personality and negotiation skills of Mrs Roosevelt. She hoped the Declaration would be a "Magna Carta of all men everywhere"— and note the word *men.* In fact, the only change we recommend be made immediately to the Declaration is to replace all the male pronouns with *he/she, him/her.*

Then, as now, the great debate was about how far international concern for human rights should be able to influence governments around the world. The Declaration neatly side-steps this issue by stating simply and boldly what human rights are, and not saying how they should be enforced.

Eleanor Roosevelt reviews her "Magna Carta of all men," New York, December 1948

The Universal Declaration of Human Rights
Part One

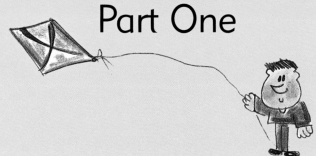

Civil and political rights

ARTICLE

1

MADE SIMPLE

When children are born, they are free and each should be treated in the same way. They have reason and conscience and should act toward one another in a friendly manner.

You may be wondering how on Earth you make people respect one another and each other's rights when so many wars are going on around the world. Well, for us the only answer is knowledge and education. If we learn about our rights and about other people and cultures, then we can live together in peace.

The key to knowing

You have need of a key to know.
Liberty of thought is the fundamental right
And education is the universal key
To unlock the knowledge and wisdom
That lies in our books and in our history.

Every child, every human being has
A right to that key, for we all have a right
To build our lives on the knowledge
Accumulated by those who lived before us.
Without that key, our world is dark and choiceless

A free world is one where every child has the
Key to a school.

Alberto Granada, 17, Colombia

Illustration by Cory Adams, USA

Everyone can claim all the rights of the Declaration, despite a different sex, a different skin color, speaking a different language, thinking different things, believing in another religion, owning more or less, being born in another social group, or coming from another country. It also makes no difference whether the country you live in is independent or not.

Some people are quick to discriminate against, or judge, anyone who seems different. Have you ever been discriminated against because of your sex or where you come from? And if you really think about it, you've probably made judgments about people based solely on their appearance!

I never knew what racism was about until I left my country

66 *When I traveled from Sierra Leone to London through Belgium, my passport was taken even though I had the necessary travel documents like everyone else. I was taken aside and interrogated while all the white people passed through easily. I was shocked and felt humiliated as a black man.*

This was the first in a series of racist encounters for me. I was staying with a family in Buntingford, a small town north of London. One evening I went for a walk around the town. After 45 minutes, a police van stopped alongside me and a policeman got out, saying, 'We have had a call reporting that a strange person was moving around.' His statement took me aback. Then I asked myself, 'Is it because I am black?'

My third encounter was late one night in London when I needed a taxi cab to take me home. Ironically, none of the taxis I stopped would take me on board. As I stood there, with the money for the fare in my pocket, I watched the white people go off home while I was left freezing in the cold. Is this racism or what? 99

Sheku Syl Kamara, 22, Sierra Leone

Illustration by Donna McCullough, USA

Racism against Gypsies in the Czech Republic

" *Like most countries, we too have to cope with racism and the hatred that goes with it. In the Czech Republic, there is a problem with Gypsies. They consider themselves to be different from the majority of the people and are determined to live as they want to.*

The "skinheads" believe that the Gypsies are wasters and thieves. They want the Gypsies to be made to leave the country. Others think that the only good Gypsy is a dead one and that they should all be hanged. Violence between these groups is on the increase; people are getting injured and even killed. Something must be done to help them understand each other. I think that racist movements should be banned, but on the other hand, the Gypsies make things worse for themselves by refusing to communicate with others. **"**

Dan Kefer, 13, Czech Republic

"Unity" by Monika Zouzelkova, 10, Czech Republic

Colors

The color of my face or my race
Red, yellow, black, or blue
All these appearances
Should cause no interferences
It really shouldn't matter to you.

Religion or my age
Shouldn't cause a rage
Education, gender, or ability
Or even my financial stability
It really shouldn't matter to you.

Equality and justice
Listen to us and trust us
To make the world peaceful
and fair;
Down with discrimination
We all must care
It all should matter to you!
Emily Mackinnon, USA

Caste system

India's 1950 Constitution grants equal status to all peoples, but caste prejudice continues.

❝ *I belong to the Newari caste. A caste is a social group to which a person belongs by birth. People from the lower castes are completely segregated from those in the higher castes. In city areas, the caste system is becoming less important. But it is more difficult to fight the caste system in the villages, where people in the higher castes do not allow people from the lower castes to enter their houses, handle their food and water, or even to touch them. The system encourages the exploitation of the lower castes by the upper castes. This is one of the most blatant violations of human rights and it hampers the development of my country.* **❞**
Urjana Shrestha, 18, Nepal

The world of women

Did you know that March 8 is International Women's Day?

Throughout history, women have usually had fewer rights and a lower social status than men. Women's movements first developed during the 1800's in the United States and Europe and then spread to other parts of the world. Women from all corners of the globe stood up for their rights as equal citizens. This first wave of feminism concentrated primarily on gaining voting rights for women.

A second wave of women's movements emerged during the 1960's, another period of great political and social change in the world. These contemporary movements have sought greater equality for women in the family, in the workplace, and in political life. Now we see women in parliament as politicians and prime ministers. It is acceptable for women to become judges, soldiers, and pilots. In fact, in areas where women are educated the standard of living rises—so everyone benefits!

Unfortunately, there is still a lot to do! On the next two pages, you can read of abuses against women, some of which have thankfully been overcome. We have come a long way, but need to travel even further.

Illustration by
Sanid Zuko, 18,
Bosnia-Herzegovina

Women and money: the Grameen Bank

We think financial independence for women is extremely important. Although many women run households, it can be very difficult for them to start up their own businesses or get paid properly for their work. Why is this? Well, it's because they often don't earn enough and so banks won't give them loans.

The Grameen Bank from Bangladesh sets out to try to solve this problem by giving women credit. The bank lends money to groups of women so that when one member of the group repays her loan, the next woman in the group receives hers. This means that the women all work together to make sure that their businesses succeed.

Each year the bank makes loans to hundreds of thousands of women in thousands of villages. Its work has given women the financial freedom they could have only dreamt of 20 years ago.

Suttee in India

Lots of people from India wanted to tell us about the cruel practice of suttee, which was once widely practiced in India. The name comes from the Sanskirt word *sati,* which means "faithful wife." According to the Hindu custom of suttee, a widow allows herself or is forced to be put to death, usually by being burned with her husband's body when it is cremated.

Scholars estimate that as many as a million women followed the custom of suttee. In 1829, the British rulers of India made suttee illegal—an example of a government recognizing an abuse and protecting an abused group.

Illustration by Jantien Roozenburg, 15, The Netherlands

A letter from Afghanistan

In Afghanistan, the Taliban, the military and political force that controls most of the country, states that girls shouldn't go to school and women can't work outside the home. Below is a letter based on one that we were sent by a girl who wishes to remain anonymous.

Dear Esther,

You said you wanted to know more about my life. Well, I can tell you because I have a lot of time to spare—too much time! I am now sitting at home as a virtual prisoner. The doors of my girls' school are shut so we can't get educated. It's as if darkness has cast a shadow over most of Afghan society, and especially on girls and women. This darkness is a regime that calls itself the Taliban. The Taliban rulers justify all their actions by saying that they are following the words of the Koran.

So we cannot go to school and we can't go outside, even to the shops, unless we are dressed in a "tent" and are accompanied by a male member of our family. We wear slippers, not high-heeled shoes, so that no one will hear us. The sound of our feet is considered offensive to the ears of men. Women have no say in social affairs or the way society is run. We sit at home like birds in a cage.

The Taliban says that women cannot work and girls cannot go to school, based on their extreme interpretation of Islamic law. The Taliban rulers do not understand what human rights are and have no respect for them. Now that all the rights of the Afghan people have been trampled on, at a national and international level we must take action. Other countries follow the laws of Islam but do not discriminate against their people in this way. Please hear our voices! Oh God, why doesn't the sun shine on the dark world of women and girls?

Anonymous

"Taliban Women" by
Arshak Sarkissian, 16, Armenia

ARTICLE

3

MADE SIMPLE

You have the right to live, and to live in freedom and safety.

When we sat down to write these pages, we soon found out that many of the editors had very different opinions about issues concerning the right to life. Some were pro-choice, others were antiabortion. Some felt that the death penalty was necessary, and others were passionately opposed.

The abortion debate

"Is it fair for a woman to have a child that she doesn't want? If a woman gets raped and becomes pregnant, is it fair for her to have a child who will remind her of that horror?"
Jantien Roozenburg, 15,
The Netherlands

"A woman who wants to have an abortion wants to kill a small child that has just begun to live."
Ali Chang, 19, Malaysia

"The right to live is the most important in our world, and for that reason we must fight against abortion."
Alberto Granada, 17,
Colombia

"You should be able to choose whether you have an abortion or not. You are the only one who can decide."
Natalia Ramirez, 12,
Argentina

Illustration by Sanid Zuko,
18, Bosnia-Herzegovina

Genocide – murdering an entire race

Throughout history, there have been attempts by one people to systematically wipe out another. This is called genocide. From the killing of indigenous peoples in the Americas and Australasia to the Nazi holocaust during World War II, the desire to completely destroy one's neighbors rears its ugly head. In the late 1800's, Ottomans and Kurds killed hundreds of thousands of Armenians. In 1915, a million Armenians died from lack of water and food or were killed by Ottomans, Kurds, or Arabs. You might think that such massacres are a thing of the past. During civil upheavals in Rwanda in 1994, some 500,000 people—mostly Tutsi—were killed by Hutu militias. Later, tens of thousands of Hutu refugees died fleeing Rwanda after a Tutsi-dominated government took control of the country. How can we, as a global community, stop this in our future?

The death penalty debate

I am against the death penalty because we as human beings have no right to take the life of the killer.
Toyin Ajasa-Oluwa, 15, UK

Suppose a thief enters your house, steals all your property, and kills your only sister. Do you think he should be imprisoned or face the death penalty?
Vladimir Popov, 14, Russia

What happens if you make a mistake? It would be terrible if you killed someone who was innocent.
Alexander Woollcombe, 17, UK

The death penalty acts as a deterrent. If people know that they will die if they kill someone, it will make them think twice before doing it.
Brian Peterson, 13, Australia

ARTICLE

4

MADE SIMPLE

Nobody has the right to treat you as his or her slave, and you should not make anyone your slave.

In history books, the word *slavery* appears all too often. Again and again, some people have decided they are masters of other people. From the 1500's to the mid-1800's, as many as 10 million Africans were taken to the Americas as slaves. The European slave drivers scarcely considered their African captives to be human at all. They beat them, chained them, and humiliated them until the slaves lost their identity. Many died of illnesses and malnutrition before they reached their destination. European slave traders were helped by some black Africans in the enslavement of others, and the slave trade enriched some African kingdoms.

William Wilberforce (1754-1833) was one of the leaders in the fight to abolish slavery in the British Empire. Shortly after his death, the Slavery Abolition Act was passed in the British Parliament. This act helped put an end to this horror. Unfortunately, slavery still exists today in many different forms, from child slavery to enforced prostitution. In some societies slavery has become so commonplace that there is little awareness that what is happening is wrong. It is time to fight against modern-day slavery, now!

A group that is helping

Working a 16- to 20-hour day, seven days a week with no holidays is certainly akin to being a slave. Kalayaan is a European coalition founded in 1987. It stands up for the rights of overworked and poorly treated workers. Often distressed workers arrive at their offices with no passport, money, or possessions!

Illustration by
Arshak Sarkissian,
16, Armenia

Child camel jockeys

Imagine you are a 6-year-old boy from India whose parents have sold you for income. You are smuggled out of the country. You are crammed with other children into a small room and fed very little. You are now a camel jockey. You are one of the many children who are kidnapped or sold and taken to wealthy countries where camel racing is a popular sport. A boy's light weight and high-pitched voice are thought to make the animals run fast.

66 *They took us and attached us with cords to the camels' backs. Those who refused or who were scared were beaten and forced on the camels. We were very frightened of falling off and dying. Children who fell could be trampled by the camels. When we got too big to be jockeys, we were returned to our countries, but many of us had forgotten where our homes and parents were.* **99**
Anonymous

Iqbal Masih

Iqbal Masih is a brave hero who risked everything and spoke out against the cruel practice of forcing children into bonded labor. This is when a child is sold to an employer in exchange for a loan of money to his or her parents. Iqbal was sold into servitude. He was enslaved at a carpet loom from the age of 4 until the age of 10, when he escaped with the support of the Bonded Labor Liberation Front (BLLF).

Iqbal received the Reebok Human Rights Youth in Action Award in December 1994 for his brave heart and hard work—he said he was "no longer afraid" of the carpet manufacturer who had owned him. Tragically, April 16, 1995, while he was cycling with two relatives in Pakistan, he was shot and killed. Nobody knows who the killer was. But the publicity his story received has spotlighted the cruelty some children are subject to, and highlighted the need to end such abuse.

Child prostitution

We heard many stories of young teen-agers, mostly girls, but some boys, who had been forced into prostitution. The majority were poor or had come from broken homes. They all needed money to survive. Lots of girls thought that they were getting jobs as waitresses, but as soon as they arrived their employers forced them to become prostitutes. They hoped that one day, when they had earned enough, they could escape their sickening life, but often this has proved impossible.

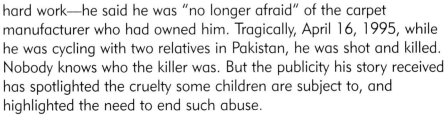

Nobody has the right to torture you.

ARTICLE
5
MADE SIMPLE

Torture is one of the most terrible of all human rights abuses. In the late 1990's, Amnesty International reported that tens of thousands of people in as many as 124 countries had been tortured. Torture is the use of physical or mental pain, often to obtain information, to punish a person, or to control the members of a group. How does this still go on? We found out from the stories sent in that torture does not only exist in war, it is also common in the home. Child abuse and family violence are both forms of torture. We must do all we can to stamp them out.

Illustration by Peter Thompson, 17, UK

Brainwashing

Brainwashing is a mental form of torture. It is a way of getting people to change their beliefs and accept as true things that they used to think were false.

Some religious sects have been accused of brainwashing their members. Many of these groups forbid new members to contact family or friends outside of the sect. This isolation has led people to say the sects put new members under mental pressure to accept the sects' beliefs.

The Medical Foundation for the Care of Victims of Torture

Victims of torture often find it difficult to make friends and to like themselves. So when Helen Bamber from the United Kingdom visited Auschwitz, a Nazi concentration camp in Poland, and met former prisoners, she decided to set up a foundation to look after torture victims.

Her foundation originally helped survivors of camps such as Auschwitz, but in the past 10 years it has helped 10,000 people from 70 countries. A team of doctors and therapists provides victims of violence with medical and social care, practical help and therapy.

ARTICLE

6

MADE SIMPLE

You should be legally protected in the same way everywhere, and like everyone else.

In 1839, a slave ship called *La Amistad* landed in America and became the subject of a famous trial. Were the African slaves on board people or property? Eventually, the U.S. Supreme Court declared that they were indeed people. Here are two more stories about people fighting for the rights to be recognized as persons.

Civil rights in America

In 1955, Rosa Parks, a black passenger on a city bus in Montgomery, Alabama, refused to give up her seat for a white person. She believed that she had as much right to sit down as the whites. She was arrested and this sparked off a protest. During this protest, called the Montgomery boycott, many blacks and whites refused to use the buses.

The undisputed leader in American civil rights was Dr. Martin Luther King, Jr. King was a tireless civil-rights campaigner, but he absolutely insisted that all protest should be without violence. In 1963, he helped organize a nonviolent march to Washington, D.C., where he said these famous words: **❝**I have a dream that my four little children will one day live in a nation where they will not be judged by the color of their skin, but by the content of their character.**❞**

These struggles led to new laws recognizing the civil rights of African Americans.

Illustration by Arshak Sarkissian, 16, Armenia

Apartheid

South Africa has been dominated by white people for about 300 years. In 1948, the ruling party decided on a policy of forced segregation or apartheid. The whites in power thought they were racially superior to the blacks, Asians, and people of mixed race. Under apartheid, people considered to be of different races were not allowed to live together, get married, or be friends. There were special bus stops, rest rooms, and beaches for each race. The whites enjoyed the riches of the country, while the others lived in poverty.

The antiapartheid movement stood up to this storm of discrimination. Many activists were killed or imprisoned, but worldwide, the movement gained strength. A boycott was organized, banning South Africa from trading and stopping them from taking part in international sporting events.

Eventually, apartheid fell in 1991. We must remember that it was the commitment of many people standing up to abuses of human rights that led to its demise. It proves that change is possible.

The law is the same for everyone;
it should be applied in the same way to all.

ARTICLE
7
MADE SIMPLE

Amnesty International has reported that dozens of the world's governments have jailed people because of their beliefs, race, gender, or ethnic origin. At trial, you should be treated fairly no matter who you are.

Nelson Mandela and "New" South Africa

In 1994, to worldwide joy and happiness, Nelson Mandela (1918-) became the first black president of South Africa. After 28 years in prison for his fight against apartheid, Mandela was released in 1990 and was asked by F. W. de Klerk, the then-President, to help put an end to this terrible period in the country's history. Their dedicated work enabled South Africa to start afresh, and for this they were both awarded the 1993 Nobel Peace Prize. In historic scenes, they organized free and fair elections, and for the first time all the people of South Africa were equally able to choose their own government.

South Africa now has a Bill of Rights so that everyone is equal before the law and equally protected by the law. It is thanks to people like Nelson Mandela that such a change came about—he is a real human rights hero.

Illustration by Aminu Seidu, Ghana

Some tribes are more equal than others

We see no reason why some tribes should be better protected by the law than others. A student who wants to remain anonymous reported to us on the escalating problems of tribalism in Kenya. He says that the ruling tribes are given better treatment than the others. The president, Daniel Toroitich arap Moi (1924-), is from the Kalenjin tribe. In 1992, there were tribal clashes in Kenya that left 2,000 people dead and many others injured and homeless. People from the Kalenjin tribe were said to have attacked other tribes. The non-Kalenjinis were arrested and locked up, while their enemies went free.

ARTICLE

8

MADE SIMPLE

You should be able to ask for legal help when the rights your country grants you are not respected.

In many countries, people disappear daily. They are kidnapped, murdered, and tortured. When this happens, the victims' families should be able to get legal help, but that's not always the case. Here is an example of one of the organizations that fights to help people find out where their missing relatives are.

Grandmothers of the "disappeared"

Marina Mansilla, 15, from Argentina heard about the many people who disappeared during the military dictatorship in Argentina in the mid-1970's. She went to visit Las Abuelas de Plaza de Mayo (Mothers of the Plaza de Mayo) to find out the truth. Las Abuelas, a famous Argentinian organization, has been working to find the real identity of the hundreds of children who were kidnapped under the regime. At the time, thousands of people who disagreed with the regime were put in concentration camps and killed. Children who were born in these camps were taken away from their mothers and given to couples who were sympathetic to the dictatorship. Over the last 20 years, Las Abuelas has identified about 60 stolen young people, 33 of whom are now with their real families. Another 13 are with good foster parents and in contact with their biological families.

Las Abuelas has been frustrated at every turn by the authorities, who refuse to assist them in their search. They have tried to find out who is responsible for this wrong-doing but have met with a wall of silence. They would like to take the case to court to find out the truth but so far have not succeeded.

Mothers and grandmothers march in the streets of Argentina, demanding that the government do more to help them in the quest to find their missing children.

Nobody has the right to put you in prison, to keep you there, or to send you away from your country unjustly, or without a good reason.

ARTICLE

9

MADE SIMPLE

Just imagine the confusion and fear of being accused of something you haven't done.

" *I was dragged out of the bus by four armed policemen to a waiting police van. I was thrown in a room for four days without my family's knowledge. I was terrified.* **"**

Anonymous, Kenya

Ugandan Asians in exile

Between 1896 and 1901, one of the first large groups of Asians arrived in Uganda from India. They served as industrial laborers, working on the British government's Uganda Railway. Over time, the Asians settled in Uganda and opened businesses.

But when Major General Idi Amin Dada seized power in 1971, there was hostility toward Ugandan Asians over economic interests. A year later, the Asians were forced to leave their land and belongings behind. Their property was confiscated by the government. It was a terrible period. Finally, in the early 1990's, the government of President Yoweri Museveni began divesting itself of confiscated Asian properties.

Illustration by Aminu Seidu, 18, Ghana

If you must go on trial this should be done in public. The people who try you should not let themselves be influenced by others.

People don't always get fair trials. You can probably find examples of this in almost any country. The law should ensure that all people are treated alike.

Ken Saro-Wiwa—injustice in Nigeria

Ken Saro-Wiwa's (1941-1995) fight to stand up for what he believed in led to his imprisonment without a fair trial and ultimately his execution in 1995. We contacted his son, Ken Wiwa, to tell us what happened.

Ken Saro-Wiwa

❝ *My father helped form the Movement for the Survival of the Ogoni People (MOSOP), an organization whose aim was to help the Ogoni people organize themselves in the peaceful defense of their lands and culture.*

On January 4, 1993, 300,000 Ogonis came surging out of their villages in support of MOSOP and the Ogoni Bill of Rights. This set down demands for a clean environment and the right to a fair share of the resources being taken from us. That day, now called Ogoni Day, marked a change of attitude among the people. My father said, 'If I had died today, I would have died a happy man.' Less than three years later, he was dead.

He was arrested in May 1994, and charged with murder. After a long trial, widely condemned by many world leaders, he was sentenced to death and hanged. Very few people doubt that my father was framed. His real crime was to draw attention to corporate greed and the human rights abuses of a regime which has pillaged a people's resources without putting anything back. He used his mental capacity to challenge his oppressors, who reacted the only way they know—with violence. Although he is dead, my father has made his point. People like you reading this article now know who the Ogoni are and what they stand for. **❞**

You should be considered innocent until it can be proved that you are guilty. If you are accused of a crime, you should always have the right to defend yourself. Nobody has the right to condemn you and punish you for something you have not done.

Everyone should be given a fair chance. It is often difficult to figure out who did what at the scene of a crime, and police everywhere make mistakes. Sometimes the people who are arrested haven't done anything wrong, so it is vital that they aren't badly treated or harassed before they are convicted. This is particularly important when you think about the effect that TV, newspapers, and the Internet can have on what we think. There have been several cases recently where the public has hounded famous people accused of committing crimes before they have got anywhere near a courtroom. The media report only one version of a story, which isn't necessarily correct.

Illustration by
Arshak Sarkissian,
16, Armenia

I am innocent until proven guilty

The policemen came to arrest me.
They locked me up,
Thrown into a small room without any light,
Although I had done nothing.
I did not know what I was charged with.
The day after, they interrogated me.
I understand it was about a robbery.
Unfortunately, my honesty made them furious.

They needed a guilty person to close the file,
And I was about to become the scapegoat.
They ordered me to get undressed,
Then they started the harsh treatment.
They whipped me, kicked me, and beat me.
For three days, they used all ways and means
To try to get a confession from me.

At one moment I wanted to give up,
Sacrifice my freedom to be left in peace.
They dishonored me, tortured me,
I could not distinguish days from nights.
On the eighth day, I was released
and the guilty arrested.
Today, I still live with the memories.
I suffered; I cannot forget.

Karim Boubred, 20, Algeria

The influence of the media

At the 1996 Olympics in Atlanta, Georgia, a security guard named Richard Jewell spotted a backpack moments before the bomb inside it exploded. At first, he was hailed a hero, but then an article appeared in the Atlanta Journal headlined "FBI searches guard's home: Man called hero after bombing under scrutiny." After that and similar headlines, Jewell was hounded by TV and newspaper reporters. As a result of the coverage, many people thought him guilty. Later, federal officials cleared him of any involvement whatsoever, but Jewell says his "name is ruined forever."

You have the right to ask to be protected if someone tries to harm your good name, enter your house, open your letters, or bother you or your family without a good reason.

Privacy means that your business is your business. You should be able to live your life without being interfered with or spied on. Daniel, our editor from Cameroon, says that in many boarding schools in his country, all letters to pupils are routinely read first by the teachers. Often prisoners in jails have their mail opened and checked, to stop them from planning escapes. In many countries, human rights activists and government opponents have their telephones bugged and their movements closely monitored. Is there ever a time when it is right to invade someone's privacy? What do you think?

"Who's watching who?!?"
by Sanid Zuko, 18,
Bosnia-Herzegovina

❝*There doesn't seem to be any kind of limit to privacy when it comes to obtaining the best story. Just look at the Royal Family in the UK. Love scandals, fake videos, and even the dreadful death of Princess Diana helped to sell huge numbers of magazines and books.*❞

Lorena Lara, 16, Argentina

Freedom of the press

Since Diana, Princess of Wales, died in a car crash as she tried to escape dozens of journalists, there has been increased discussion about people's right to privacy. Should the press have freedom to print what they like? What about famous people? They often seek publicity, but should the press be allowed to take photos of them wherever they go?

You have the right to come and go as you wish within your country. You have the right to leave your country to go to another one; and you should be able to return to your country if you want.

ARTICLE

13

MADE SIMPLE

In Berlin, Germany, in 1989, there was an enormous celebration and thousands came together to tear down the wall that had divided their city for so long. For many, the Berlin Wall had come to symbolize a barrier to their freedoms—and with its destruction, East and West Germany became united once more. In 1991, when the USSR dissolved, millions of people could do what they had dreamed of doing for most of their lives. They could travel.

Most people take for granted the fact that they can travel or live anywhere they like in their own country, but in some countries this basic human right is still not respected. We researched the following stories about Cyprus and North Korea.

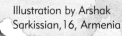

Illustration by Arshak Sarkissian,16, Armenia

Cyprus

Ever since 1974, there has been no freedom of movement between north and south on the island of Cyprus. Turkish Cypriots live in the north and Greek Cypriots live in the south. Most young Cypriots have never met anyone from "the other side." The capital, Nicosia, is also divided.

"*We listen to the same songs, we watch the same movies, we love the same land. It's about time they stopped treating us as different.***"**

Constantina Georgiou, 15, Cyprus

North Korea

Traveling in The Democratic People's Republic of Korea (North Korea) is not as easy as in some countries. The state runs the entire transportation system. Almost all cars are government-owned and are intended for official business use. The only people who are allowed to leave the country are officials and certain favored artists, academics, or athletes.

If someone hurts you, you have the right to go to another country and ask it to protect you. You lose this right if you have killed someone and if you, yourself, do not respect what is written here.

Imagine being persecuted, being forced out of your home, leaving all your favorite possessions, not knowing if you might see your home again. It's a terrifying thought. But that's not the end of it. Imagine trying to get asylum. Imagine arriving in a foreign country, where nobody cares about you, where you have no money, no friends, where you can't speak the language and have no idea what will happen to you tomorrow. And even when you get permission to stay, you have to rebuild your life. Unfortunately, there are about 30 million refugees in the world. This is twice as many as there were in 1985! When you next meet a refugee, think about what they have been through.

Equal chance
Refugees are normal.
They are no different
from anyone else.
They should be treated
normally and equally.
Racism against refugees must stop.

Everyone has
an equal right to education.
Because of language problems
and what they have been through,
refugees should receive special help
to give them an equal chance.
This help should be
fair and equal for all refugees.

It should not separate or divide
refugees from other students.
All support for refugees should aim
to make them feel
a normal part of the class,
where everyone has an equal
chance and is treated
fairly and equally.

Refugees are normal.
Refugees are welcome here.
We're all different,
but we're all equal.

Pupils from George Mitchell School, UK, wrote this poem together.

Illustration submitted by the Human Rights Education Programme, Pakistan

Here are some episodes from the life of a young Kurdish refugee who had to flee from Turkey.

September 4th, 1997

Dear Diary,

Today my father was killed in the marketplace before my eyes. The soldiers shot him three times in the chest, and he died instantly.

There was nothing that I could do but cry. My father was dead.

September 7th, 1997

Dear Diary,

The soldiers came to the house and I had to hide. Never in my life have I felt so much fear. I crouched in a small cupboard under the stairs for two hours until they left. Many of my neighbors and friends were killed. I realized that I had to leave this country before something terrible happened to me.

September 10th, 1997

Dear Diary,

I left with very little luggage because I didn't want the soldiers to know I was going. When I arrived at the airport it was very noisy, and as I boarded the flight, I knew I was finally free.

September 11th, 1997

Dear Diary,

When I got off the plane, I was told to go into a small waiting room full of people. The sign above the door said "Detention Centre waiting room." I waited in the room for two hours, then finally my name was called. I was taken into another small waiting room, where I was asked questions about why I left my country. Finally, I was driven by van to a massive building marked DETENTION CENTRE. I had no idea that it would be like this. My troubles seemed far from over.

You have the right to belong to a country and nobody can prevent you, without a good reason, from belonging to another country if you wish.

A dictionary definition of nationality is "a people having a common origin, tradition, and language and capable of forming or actually constituting a nation-state." But there is much more to nationality than just this. It means a certain way of life, with your own festivals, languages, national anthem, and special native costumes to wear.

Nationality also refers to the fact that many people continue the habits, customs, and language of their native land when they go to live someplace else. In many cities in the United States, there are groups of people who try to keep alive the customs and traditions of other countries.

Kosovo

One of the members of our editorial committee comes from Kosovo, a troubled province of Serbia. (Serbia is one of the two republics that make up the Federal Republic of Yugoslavia.) She gave us the following report.

In 1989, Serbia ended the *autonomy* (self-rule) of Kosovo. About 90 percent of the people of Kosovo are Albanians. The Kosovo Albanians voted for independence in a 1991 referendum. In 1992, they elected a president and parliament. Serbia declared the referendum and elections illegal.

Over the last 10 years, Albanians have formed a parallel system of schools, government, and funding. They tried to keep out of the Bosnian war by resisting peacefully. But there have been repeated atrocities as Serbs and Albanians have clashed. Diplomatic negotiations have broken down, and many say they will fight until they win their independence.

Young Kosovo Albanians on a march to protest for the right to have their own country

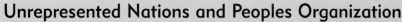

Unrepresented Nations and Peoples Organization

Unrepresented Nations and Peoples Organization (UNPO) was created by nations and peoples who are not represented in organizations like the UN. Founded in 1991, UNPO has about 50 member organizations representing over 100 million people denied their nationality. They are struggling to regain their lost countries, to preserve their cultural identities, to protect their basic human and economic rights, and to safeguard the natural environment.

The following groups currently belong to UNPO:

● Abkhasia ● Aborigines of Australia ● Acheh ● Albanians in Macedonia ● Assyria ● Bashkortostan ● Batwa ● Bougainville ● Buryatia ● Chameria ● Chechen Republic Ichkeria ● Chittagong Hill Tracts ● Chuvash ● Circassians ● Cordillera ● Crimean Tatars ● East Timor ● East Turkestan ● Gagauzia ● Greek Minority in Albania ● Hungarian Minority in Romania ● Ingushetia ● Inkeri ● Iraqi Turkoman ● Kalahui, Hawaii ● Karenni State ● Komi ● Kosovo ● Kurdistan (Iraq) ● Lakota Nation ● Maohi People ● Mapuche ● Mari ● Mon People ● Nagaland ● Ogoni ● Republic of South Moluccas ● Sakha Republic (Yakutia) ● Sanjak ● Scania ● Taiwan ● Tartarstan ● Tibet ● Tuva ● Udmurt ● West Papua ● Zanzibar

An unrepresented person appeals to her oppressor

I look at myself in the mirror,
I don't like what I see.
But there's no way I'm going to stop knocking
On all those walls built in front of me.

I don't want to whine,
I don't want to make you cry,
I just want to make you care,
I just want to make you try.

What is it exactly that you mind about me?
Is it the language that I speak?
Is it the color of my blood?
Is it the purity of my heart?
or maybe you mind ME in OUR part.

I'm not a marionette for them to play with,
I want to burn these ropes that hurt so much.
Stop reminding me that I'm not allowed to,
Stop forbidding my education,
Stop ignoring my self-determination.

Stop making me flee,
I'm not here to fight:
I'm here to stop fighting
Because I've seen it on TV,
That war is the worst way to get free.

Jeta Xharra, 20, Kosovo, Yugoslavia

"Flags" by Gözde Boğa, 15, Turkey

The Universal Declaration of Human Rights

Part Two

Economic, social, and cultural rights

Illustration opposite: by Anonymous, UK

As soon as a person is legally entitled, he or she has the right to marry and have a family. In doing this, neither the color of your skin, the country you come from, nor your religion should be impediments. Men and women have the same rights when they are married and also when they are separated. Nobody should force a person to marry. The government of your country should protect your family and its members.

Many countries have granted women equal rights with men in matters of marriage, divorce, and family property. But in some places, girls are forced to marry when they are still children. These child brides have limited opportunities in life and are often stuck in a web of poverty. Marriage should be a choice.

Multiple marriages

Do you think it's wrong to have more than one wife? Polygamy, which means having more than one wife, is common among Uganda's Ankole people. When a man takes another wife, he often doesn't have the means to support more than one family. This can lead to neglect of wives and children, and quarreling and unhappiness in the home.

Gifts

In certain cultures, marriage involves a gift from the family of the bride or groom to the other family. In many societies, for example, the bride's family gives money or property to the groom or his family. Such a gift is called a dowry. In other cultures, the groom and his family present gifts to the family of the bride.

Illustration by Zuzana Zuzna, 11, Czech Republic

66 *One of the biggest evils in Indian society is the dowry system. This means that if the bride does not bring any dowry from her parents' house, the bride is harassed, tortured, or sometimes even burned alive. It is high time we got rid of the evil practice of dowry taking. Boys should refuse to take a dowry, and girls should firmly say no to greedy bridegrooms. Thus, the evil system would be put to an end. SAY NO TO DOWRY.* **99**
Surabhi Maru, India

66 *In Uganda, forced marriage can take place. A man comes and he says, 'Give me your daughter, and I'll give you five cows.' If the father agrees, the man takes the girl.* **99**
Sarah Nalubwama, Uganda

66 *Marriage is associated with happiness and responsibility, and it's a symbol of maturity. The issue of forced marriage does not exist in our society, and once a couple gets married, we hope they live a happy life with their kids. Marriage is one of the greatest things in life.* **99**
Alfred Syl Kamara, 15, Sierra Leone

You have the right to own things, and nobody has the right to take these from you without a good reason.

Imagine how you would feel if your family had lived in one place for centuries, and then someone came along and claimed your home as theirs. We've heard and read about many people whose property has been taken away from them.

The Australian Aborigines

Similar to settlers in the United States and Canada, the Europeans who came to Australia thought that their race and culture were superior. When the British colonized Australia in 1788, they killed thousands of Aborigines. Wild land and desert areas were cultivated and mined. The Aborigines lost many of their sacred sites and could no longer live as they had done for centuries.

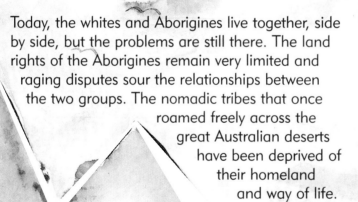

Today, the whites and Aborigines live together, side by side, but the problems are still there. The land rights of the Aborigines remain very limited and raging disputes sour the relationships between the two groups. The nomadic tribes that once roamed freely across the great Australian deserts have been deprived of their homeland and way of life.

And what about Palestine?

Both the Arabs and Israelis strongly believe that they have rights to the same land. Palestinian Arabs who had lived in their homes and villages for thousands of years saw them disappear when the state of Israel was created. In 1947, the UN divided Palestine into a Jewish state and an Arab state. In 1948, it created Israel—without consulting the Palestinians. Many people think that since then, Arab property rights have been consistently abused, but the Jewish Israelis think it's their homeland, too.

Settlers in the United States and Canada thought that their race and culture were superior to those of the indigenous peoples. As a result, much of the indigenous culture has been destroyed.

Guatemala's Indians

In Latin America, many countries have tried to improve Indian welfare. However, many disputes arose in the 1980's and 1990's. Government leaders frequently complained that the Indians lacked respect for national policies. The Indians charged that the governments allowed their lands to be damaged by agriculture, industry, or mining. A serious clash occurred in Guatemala. Thousands of Indians there died, and thousands of others fled to refugee camps in Mexico. Rigoberta Menchú (1959-), a Mayan Indian, won the 1992 Nobel Peace Prize for her efforts to gain equal rights for Guatemala's Indians.

66 *Poor people can't own proper houses. So they build humble cottages in the outskirts of cities. However, the rich want to disperse the poor and make money by building new luxury houses. Very often, the rich hire civilian service corps and let them do bad things to those who won't leave their homes. ... These are real things in Korea. All people have rights to have their own roofs.* 99

Sarangbang Group for Human Rights, South Korea

Illustrations by
Sanid Zuko, 18,
Bosnia-Herzegovina

ARTICLE
18
MADE SIMPLE

You have the right to profess your religion freely, to change it, and to practice it either on your own or with other people.

Think of all the people who have put forward ideas about how the world was created, or what happens after we die, or what is the best way to run a country. Who is right? How do we know? There's no right or wrong answer. Isn't it, therefore, wrong to persecute people for their beliefs? Isn't it wrong to stop someone from practicing his or her religion? From the Christian crusades to the shooting of supporters of democracy in Tiananmen Square, Beijing, China, people have suffered for what they believe. Religion has long divided the people of Northern Ireland into rival groups, sometimes resulting in violence. When will this end?

Ngawang Sangdrol, prisoner of conscience

Would you go to prison for your religion?

A Tibetan nun, Ngawang Sangdrol, did in August 1990, when she was only 13 years old. She and other Buddhist nuns from the Garu monastery went to a demonstration calling for Tibetan independence. Ngawang was arrested, and even though she was too young to be tried, she was held prisoner for nine months.

She was arrested in Lhasa in 1992 for demonstrating and was sentenced to three years imprisonment. While in prison, Ngawang and 12 other Buddhist nuns sang uplifting Tibetan protest songs. She was given six more years in prison! Amnesty International and The Body Shop Foundation are two groups lobbying for her release. The Body Shop Foundation, established in 1989, gathers funds for social, human, animal, and environmental welfare issues.

Illustration by Sanid Zuko,
18, Bosnia-Herzegovina

Archbishop Desmond Tutu: Antiapartheid hero

We asked contributors to this book to interview their human rights heroes. Yolande van Rensburg and Bushra Razock from South Africa interviewed Archbishop Desmond Tutu (1931-   ) to find out his ideas about religion and human rights. Tutu won the 1984 Nobel Peace Prize for his nonviolent campaign against apartheid. He said:

Yolande van Rensburg and Bushra Razock with Archbishop Tutu

"A country that has no religion would be an extremely weird country. We are created to be religious, and being religious really means being open to the mysterious, to the holy, to the good, and to the beautiful. It would be a very, very sad day if there was no space for religion. I myself would say that South Africa should not claim to be a religious, Christian country. It should be a country that says it is secular, secular in the sense that the government does not try to impose one religious view on its people. We have a diversity of religions in our country, and there should be a rule for all of them. Everyone can think whatever they want. Everyone has the right to freedom of thought. We ought to make it possible for our country to respect other religions, and just to say that as a government we allow freedom of religion, which is a constitutional right."

ARTICLE

19

MADE SIMPLE

You have the right to think what you want, to say what you like, and nobody should forbid you from doing so. You should be able to share your ideas also—with people from any other country.

"Oh, you can't say that." How many times has somebody said that to you? If you're sitting there thinking that nobody has, then you are a very lucky person. Over the centuries, lots of people have been prevented from saying what they think. Artists and writers in particular have experienced this problem, as many controversial pictures and books have been burned. You might think that it's always wrong to destroy or censor someone else's work, but think again. What do you feel about people who put pornography or racist literature on the Internet? Should they be allowed to do this, or should such material be banned?

A sound unheard

You hear me cry,
You hear me mutter.
But still it doesn't really matter.
I try to scream,
I try to speak,
But you still control my speech.
This determination in my voice;
This persistence to continue till I believe;
My right to freedom of speech.
Freedom of expression is my vision,
That one day we will no longer dream,
but live a successful fantasy.
Which is blinded in the clouds of reality.

Toyin Ajasa-Oluwa, 15, UK

Aung San Suu Kyi: 1991 Nobel Peace Prize Winner

Aung San Suu Kyi (1945-) led her National League for Democracy party to victory in elections in Burma in 1990. The results were ignored by the military government, who had earlier gunned down students campaigning for democracy in Rangoon. Ms Suu Kyi was placed under house arrest, but she continued her nonviolent struggle for democracy and human rights. Her period of house arrest ended in 1995, but the military still watch her constantly and tap her phone. She is not allowed to meet with her supporters. She says, "The regaining of my freedom has in turn imposed a duty on me to work for the freedom of the other women and men who have suffered far more—and who continue to suffer far more—than I have." Why does she do this when she could get on a plane and leave? It's because of her passionate belief in the freedom to say what she pleases and the freedom to protest against the tyranny of the military regime.

" *When my family eats together in the evening, I'm not allowed to say anything. It's not because I don't have anything to say, it's because I'm the youngest. I often sit there and listen to the conversation and I want to say something, but I can't. Only my eldest brother is allowed to talk. Why can't I have the chance to talk?* **"**
Richard Mbembe, 17,
Nigeria

" *Last week I read in the newspaper about someone who had been put in prison for saying something against his government. This is so wrong. Everyone should be able to think and say what they like, as long as they aren't lying. If you believe something from the bottom of your heart—say it and don't be afraid.* **"**
Liam O'Neill, 13,
Ireland

" *It makes me so mad when people don't take me seriously. Just because I'm young doesn't mean I haven't got anything worthwhile to say. Not only should I have freedom of expression, I should also have the right to be listened to!!!* **"**
Juan da Silva, 17, Peru

"Gagged" by Damien Boltauzer, 13,
Canada

51

ARTICLE
20
MADE SIMPLE

You have the right to organize peaceful meetings or to take part in meetings in a peaceful way. It is wrong to force someone to belong to a group.

Meeting is one of the most important things we do. Meeting with others enables us to share ideas, make decisions, and plan our lives. In some countries, people are prevented by the authorities from holding a meeting or forming an association. Why? What are the authorities afraid of?

Students in South Korea

We have received reports from South Korean students who say that they are prevented by the police and the government from holding certain political meetings and organizing peaceful demonstrations. Many of them have been arrested because of their alleged association with North Korea. They would like to see a unified Korea, but they cannot form associations and often have their meetings disrupted. Yang Hyon Cha, a student who went to the World Youth Festival in Cuba in 1997, tells us she was arrested on her return because it was supposed that she had been meeting with North Koreans.

Illustration by Damien Boltauzer, 13, Canada

Illustration by Michael Heequaye, Ghana

52

Bhima Sangha

In many countries, young children work. Many people and governments agree that this must stop, but in the meantime, we think that these children need employment rights. We heard about the Bhima Sangha, which is a union made up entirely of working children in India. They are not officially allowed to be a union, and they face resistance from their employers and even their parents, but they still think it is important to meet. They want to protect their rights as workers now, but just as important, want to stop child labor in the future.

Illustration border by Urjana Shrestha, 18, Nepal

The children of the Bhima Sangha wrote and told us how the union started.

66 *In a small village lived a family. The children, Ravi and Radha, worked hard helping their parents and were domestic helps in other homes. They were very keen to go to school, but they never had time.*

As Ravi grew older he started working in the city. There he met Bhimanna, an activist involved in helping working children. Bhimanna said, 'I work with children like you. We will tell you how unions help children and we will also teach you certain life skills.'

Ravi was very happy and told his friend Girish the good news. They went to Bhimanna's union to find out more, and then decided to get together with some working children. To begin with, only a few children joined them. They encouraged more children to come by playing games for half an hour, and then talking to them about their problems.

The children asked, 'What can we do about our problems?' Ravi said, 'If we want to find a solution to our problems, then we need to get together and build our own union—the Bhima Sangha. If we do this with determination, we can build a new world. Let this be our plan for the future. 99

ARTICLE

21

MADE SIMPLE

You have the right to take part in your country's political affairs either by belonging to the government yourself or by choosing politicians who have the same ideas as you. Governments should be voted for regularly, and voting should be secret. You should get a vote and all votes should be equal. You also have the same right to join the public service as anyone else.

Most governments today say that they are democratic. But many lack some essential freedoms usually associated with democracy. In some countries, for example, the people are not allowed freedom of speech or the right to vote.

The following views explain democracy as a form of government, a way of life, and a goal or ideal. Views on the benefits of rule by law have been expressed since democracy began to develop in ancient Greece as early as the 600's B.C.

"Right to vote" by Virginia Rivilli, Ariadna Silva, Carla Spagnolo, Paula Daveloza, all from Argentina

Democracy may not work perfectly, but it seems to be the best form of government. If people are free to vote as they please, without being pressured or bribed, it ensures the system of government the majority wants. A good democracy makes public services, health, and schooling available for everyone—not just for a privileged few.

> 66 *The basis of a democratic state is liberty.* 99
> Aristotle

> 66 *As I would not be a slave, so I would not be a master. This expresses my idea of democracy. Whatever differs from this, to the extent of the difference, is no democracy.* 99
> Abraham Lincoln

> 66 *Government of the people, by the people, for the people, still remains the sovereign definition of democracy.* 99
> Sir Winston Churchill

> 66 *Democracy ... is the only form of government that is founded on the dignity of man, not the dignity of some men, of rich men, of educated men, or of white men, but of all men.* 99
> Robert Maynard Hutchins

Dictators—A rogues gallery

There are a lot of governments that pay lip-service to democracy but that are in fact dictatorships. Elections are rigged and corrupt, while human rights are ignored. Over the years, there have been notorious dictators in various countries around the world. Here are a few notables.

Who? Adolf Hitler (1889-1945)—Germany
When? Ruled from 1933-1945
What? Hitler believed that the Germans were the "master race." He hated Jews, homosexuals, Gypsies, and anyone who refused to obey him. He sent millions of Jews and others to concentration camps.

Who? Pol Pot (1925-1998)—Cambodia
When? Ruled from 1975-1978/1979
What? There is evidence that during his rule, hundreds of thousands of Cambodians died in "the killing fields." There they were executed or overworked. Many others died of starvation.

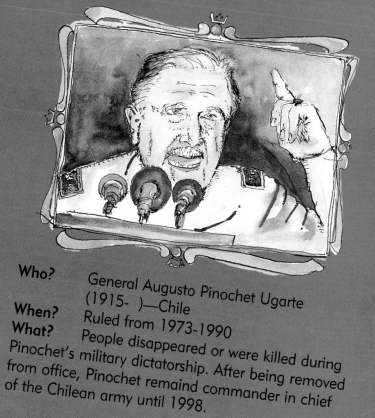

o? Major General Idi Amin Dada (1925?-)—Uganda
en? Ruled from 1971-1979
t? Many thousands of Ugandans who greed with Amin's policies were killed, at his r or by his supporters.

Who? General Augusto Pinochet Ugarte (1915-)—Chile
When? Ruled from 1973-1990
What? People disappeared or were killed during Pinochet's military dictatorship. After being removed from office, Pinochet remaind commander in chief of the Chilean army until 1998.

Illustrations by Sanid Zuko, 18, Bosnia-Herzegovina

55

ARTICLE

22

MADE SIMPLE

The society in which you live should help you to develop and to make the most of all the advantages (culture, work, social welfare) which are offered to you and to all the men and women in your country.

Did you know that on average people are living much longer than they did at the beginning of the century—by about 30 years? We are better fed, healthier, better educated, and we have more access to clean drinking water and less exposure to fatal diseases. The disease smallpox has been eliminated from the whole world. Polio has been nearly eliminated in developed countries. For many people in many countries, life is dignified, healthy, and full.

Progress must continue

Although life is good for many, sadly the number of people living in absolute poverty, with no access to any kind of social security, has in fact risen. The UN and most Western governments have pledged time and time again to eliminate poverty from our Earth, and we know that it is possible. We all think it's just a matter of making a plan and putting it into action. We must fight to make it happen!

"A world with healthcare and a world without"
by Urjana Shrestha, 18, Nepal

" *If you're a baby born in Gambia, the odds against your surviving are high because of poor delivery techniques, common infectious diseases, and unclean water.* **"**
Kumba Ndure, 19, Gambia

" *In Kenya, two patients often have to share a bed, sleeping head to toe.* **"**
John Atwiambo, 17, Kenya

Illustration submitted
by the Human Rights
Education Programme,
Pakistan

57

ARTICLE

23

MADE SIMPLE

You have the right to work, to be free to choose your work, to get a salary that allows you to live and support your family. If a man and a woman do the same work, they should get the same pay. All people who work have the right to join together to defend their interests.

There's one major problem here. If there are no jobs around, who can guarantee you the right to work? Similarly, in a poor country, how can the government pay everyone unemployment benefits and supplements if there is no money for basic health care? A government can make laws to ensure that men and women get equal pay for equal work, which is only fair. But it is more difficult to guarantee work. This is why we feel we need to become more creative about work. If jobs do not exist, we should see how we can build small businesses to meet the needs of the local community, businesses that are profitable but also eco-friendly and sustainable. Maybe also if there isn't enough work to go around we need to learn how to share the jobs that do exist.

Child labor rights

This is an extremely difficult issue – should children have the right to work? In the UK, no child under 14 may work legally, even part-time. But in some developing countries, children may be the major breadwinners in a family! How can a global human right be written to cover the needs of all countries?

Some people feel that child labor is so terrible that it should be stopped immediately. Others say that if you did this, life would become much worse for the families who depend on their children's wages. Somehow we have to find a way to make sure that all children have the opportunity to receive schooling and to enjoy free time. If all children had compulsory free education for at least part of the day, then they would have a chance to get a better job and climb out of the poverty trap in which they find themselves.

Illustrations submitted by the
Human Rights Education Programme, Pakistan

Equal pay for equal work

In the United States in the late 1990's, a white woman earned on average 74 cents for every dollar earned by a man, while an African American woman earned 65 cents? Many women think it deeply unfair and participated in an Equal Pay Day, where 107 women's groups demonstrated for equal pay. The Paycheck Fairness Act was introduced in the U.S. Congress in 1998. It would provide improved legal remedies for women who are not being paid equal wages to do equal work.

Illustration by Urjana Shrestha, 18, Nepal

Watchdog on trade union rights!

Question: Who watches over trade union rights?
Answer: The International Labor Organization (ILO), in Geneva, Switzerland. The ILO helps trade unions and workers stop exploitation. Joining a trade union, which is an association that looks after the rights of workers, is often the only way that an individual can stand up to the might of a big company. The ILO has set up a Commission of Inquiry to look at places where trade union rights have been abused. Recently, it has found problems in Colombia and Sudan, where trade unionists are frequently imprisoned or mysteriously disappear.

ARTICLE

24

MADE SIMPLE

Each work day should not be too long, since everyone has the right to rest and should be able to take regular paid holidays.

Everybody needs time off. Many of us take this right for granted, and for us, going shopping, going to the movies, or playing sports is part of everyday life. Unfortunately, there are millions of people around the world who are unable to enjoy leisure time. Those in bonded labor are treated as slaves and are not allowed time to relax. In some societies, women can't leave the house and are forbidden from taking part in sports and other social activities. Disabled people, orphans, and mentally handicapped people are locked away in some parts of the world. Obviously, they deserve to live a fun and fulfilling life, too.

"The Right to Play" by Mia Rivera, 11, Philippines

Too much work can kill

During our editorial meeting, we were visited by a professor from Korea, who told us about the education system in the Far East. She said that in many countries, such as South Korea and Japan, children don't get much time to play. A typical day can start at 7 a.m. Children are at school by 8 a.m. and work hard until 4 p.m., with just a 20-minute break for lunch. At home, a student may do two hours of homework, until 7 p.m., go to private classes until 10 p.m., and then fit in another hour of homework before bedtime. Many children are not allowed to watch TV or enjoy free time. The professor told us, **"***Children who live in these countries don't know how to play, they don't know how to rest. This pressure is too much for a child. In fact, already there are stories of 16-year-olds who have committed suicide because they can't stand the pressure.***"**

"I've got a holiday on the 15th of August, for me that is freedom."
Anonymous, India

Illustration by Melina C. D'Auria, 15, Argentina

You have the right to have whatever you need so that you and your family: do not fall ill; do not go hungry; have clothes and a house; and are helped if you are out of work, if you are ill, if you are old, if your wife or husband is dead, or if you do not earn a living for any other reason you cannot help.

Homelessness is a major world problem, especially in large cities. Many of the victims living on the streets are children. Sometimes they have run away from home because they have suffered abuse. Often they are there because their families can't afford to feed them. Some of them beg. Others illegally sell matches or flowers, or clean car windows. In Mexico City, many live on the outskirts and travel for an hour and a half to get to the fashionable Pink Zone, where they clean the windows of luxury cars for a couple of coins.

" *I want to go to school to learn things and to play with other kids. I wish I wasn't poor and I didn't have to work.* **"**

Guadalupe, 5, Mexico

"Homeless" by Georgina Barrows, 15, UK

" *I am a seventh-grade student living in Pakistan. Even though I'm still young, I can see things that I know could be changed if someone cared. Poverty is a very big issue. Most of the population does not have proper homes. The poor make their houses from cloth and straw. Some people sleep and live on the sidewalk. I think maybe no one cares now, but perhaps my generation will care and make my country better for everyone, because everyone has a right to a home.* **"**

Naiha Ali, 13, Pakistan

Opposite: "Boy in the Rubble"
by Ruth Hardwicke, 16, UK

From the streets to the university

" I started living on the streets of Bogotá, Colombia, when I was only 7 years old. I left home to live in the gutters because my family couldn't afford to feed me. Over three years, I learned all about poverty and I saw firsthand the cruelty of Bogotá society.

People hated us. At night, a drunk taxi driver would get angry and shoot at us. If a gang didn't like you, they would kill you. The police used to beat me and my friends frequently, just because we were living on the streets and begging for money. To survive on the streets there are just two laws: the law of strength and the law of silence.

When I went to sleep, I never knew whether I would wake up again. I knew the violence of the night in Bogotá, I saw the alcoholics, the homeless, and the prostitutes beside me. Every day someone was dying next to me. I was just a child, but I grew up very fast.

I was 10 years old when the Fundación Niños de los Andes took me off the streets and gave me the chance to study and a place to sleep. Now it is six years. I want to finish my studies, go to the university, and get money to help my family. I have three small brothers, and I don't want them ever to live on the streets. Now that I have a future, I want to work with street children who don't yet know they have a future. "

Alberto Granada, 17, Colombia

ARTICLE
26
MADE SIMPLE

You have the right to go to school and everyone should go to school. Primary schooling should be free. You should be able to learn a profession or continue your studies as far as you wish. At school, you should be able to develop all your talents and you should be taught to get on with others, whatever their race, religion, or the country they come from. Your parents have the right to choose how and what you will be taught at school.

Even though we don't always enjoy every aspect of school, we all agree it's a good thing! The movement toward universal education had its beginnings in Europe in the early to mid-1800's. Free and compulsory education became well established in most developed countries by the early 1900's. In other places, cultural, social, and political issues have been obstacles to universal education.

Nowadays, most governments worldwide are increasing resources for education. The situation is improving, but exclusion from education by culture, politics, and gender continues. Education is a vital factor in advancing a person's and a community's economic and social well-being.

"Going to school" by Aya Balde, Democratic Republic of the Congo

Illustration by Srijana Shrestha, 15, Nepal

Education in Baluchistãn

In Baluchistãn, Pakistan, there is an acute shortage of female teachers because most adult women in the area have not been educated properly. Parents, however, only want their daughters to be taught by women, and so they are reluctant to send their daughters to school. This means that girls still don't receive a decent education.

The Baluchistãn Primary Education Programme was set up to address this problem. It does this by letting the parents choose young women from the village to be trained as teachers. Parents are happier and show more interest in the benefits of education. More than 200 of these schools have been created since 1992. A way has been found to respect the villagers' right to retain their own culture while at the same time giving their young girls the right to education.

ARTICLE

27

MADE SIMPLE

Everyone has the right to participate freely in the cultural life of the community, to enjoy the arts, and to share in and benefit from scientific advances. Equally, everyone has the right to protect the copyright of their scientific, literary, or artistic work.

What is culture? Culture is the life-blood of a nation. It is a country's music, literature, film, theater, fashion, and customs. There is a danger now that TV and music from the richest countries, with all the marketing and hype they receive, will wipe out smaller national cultures. When a nation loses its life-blood, its heart stops beating. So we have a duty to keep alive the cultures of small nations.

What is copyright? If you write a song, you don't want someone else to say that it was his or her idea and pocket all the proceeds. By owning the copyright, you protect your work. You can copyright things, such as poems, novels, photographs, and computer programs. Similar protection for an object you invent is called a patent. Sometimes, these ownership laws are not well respected, as the following story shows.

Ripping off the rain forest

The tourist in jeans and sunglasses watched as the man in the loincloth heated a sliver of bark over an open fire. He saw him scrape off the bubbles of paste with a dry twig and spread them on the child's wound. Almost at once the bleeding stopped and a film of new skin spread across it.

Later, on the plane, the tourist looked at the sample of paste in front of him and wondered where his friend in the loincloth would sleep tonight? Probably on a bed of leaves. He thought of his own house with the two cars in the garage, the big-screen TV, and the warm, comfortable bed, and he wondered, "Is this fair?"

In the boardroom, the managing director congratulated him on the wonder drug and said it was going to make millions! "I know," said the man, "But can't we give some of it to the forest people who taught us how to make it?"

"Ha! Ha! Ha!" The laughter echoed in the man's ears as he crept away, feeling like a thief.

A small group of the editors of this book wrote this story together.

Illustration by Arshak Sarkissian, 16, Armenia

ARTICLE

MADE SIMPLE

So that your rights will be respected, there must be an "order" that can protect them. This "order" should be local and worldwide.

If we all wrote down three things that would make a free and fair world, in which all rights can be fully realized, everyone's list would be different. But all of the editors working on this book agree on this point—that every human being has the right to live in peace and security without fear of war or other forms of oppression.

We, children of the tragedy,
We bear inside undressable wounds.
We bear a history of dehumanized humanity
In Algeria or in Bosnia, in Rwanda or Uganda...
How many are we? Tens, thousands...
Whose lives have been taken,
Whose dreams have been stolen,
Whose rights have been violated.
We live in a city where there is confusion,
Where the blood flows,
Where horror and terror are sown,
Where arbitrariness is as powerful as the law.

We, children of the tragedy,
We need to be relieved,
To be protected, loved, and guided...
We bear inside the fate of Humanity,
Dare to transform our tragedy
Into a symphony of peace and fraternity.
At least respect the declarations you signed,
The Human Rights Declaration is an eternal guide.
Mohammed, 18, Algeria

"I'm too young to die" by Ella Hewitt, 10, UK

The laws of every organized society make up a complex pattern of balanced freedoms and restrictions. Some people think of laws as the natural enemies of freedom. But actually, the law both limits and protects freedom. For example, it forbids violent acts against others and in doing so allows others to live securely and in peace.

Illustration by Anonymous, UK

In the territory of South Ossetia

War had troubled the Republic of Georgia beginning in 1991. In 1992, it intensified in the town of Ts'khinvali, in the South Ossetia region. This is one girl's experiences.

"I was a little girl of about 8 when the war began. At first we were not afraid because we couldn't believe that war could really happen. Next morning, the streets of Ts'khinvali were full of policemen and citizens with automatic guns. It was terrible. At night, the houses burned. Nobody could do anything. We were helpless. My mother hid us under the bed. I looked at my parents and saw fear in their faces. I could hear only one word — 'War!'

The town had always been friendly. Many nationalities lived together happily—Russians, Ossetians, Georgians, Armenians, and Jewish people. My best friend was called Georgi. We played together and loved each other very much. One day I heard a terrible explosion. I was told that Georgi had been killed at home by his father's grenades. I cried bitterly. We left three days later, with tears in our eyes.

Children don't need grenades, bombs, and guns. Children want to be happy with their parents and friends. They need blue sky, sunshine, and freedom. I don't want anybody to die. Children must have the right to be free and to study without their schools and homes being bombed. I have no desire to hear bombs and see children dying. Never!! Nowhere!!!"

Anonymous, Republic of Georgia

The pit

" *I went to a place, near Bihać, Bosnia-Herzegovina, to visit a pit called by the local people the Abyss, or the infinite pit. During the aggression in my country, the Serbs have thrown around 300 people into the pit. Only half have been identified. I stare at the pit. It is terrible! It is awful! The infinite pit.* **"**

The infinite pit, the infinite pit,
Feelings are frozen, time has stopped.
Instead of flowers,
Scattered bones on the fields.
You can hear laughter and happiness
Only as inarticulate screams of pain,
Suddenly everything is closed, buried.
Life and time and laughter and
Happiness and tears.
Somewhere inside the people
There is a flame of fear,
Restlessness and darkness.
I am ashamed to be a human being,
That I am born and that I am living.
If we were hyenas
We would have more mercy,
Humanity and sense.
Rights?! Who is talking about rights?!
What are they? Do they exist at all?
I was a child, I was happy.
I was a human being
And I was happy to be alive,
To be able to grow up.
I wanted to leave descendants,
To contribute to the development
Of the human race.
Now I ask myself, does it make sense?
Or did the sense in living disappear
The moment a dozen children,
Men and women were killed,
Into the infinite pit they were thrown.
I was a child!
They interrupted my childhood!
I ran after the butterflies,
But I caught up with the killers!

Jasmin Salkic, 17, Bosnia-Herzegovina

Illustration by Emma Crake, UK

69

You have duties toward the community within which your personality can only fully develop. The law should guarantee human rights. It should allow everyone to respect others and to be respected.

We think this Article means that we are all responsible for making sure that each other's rights are protected. These rights weren't written for only heads of government and industry to enforce. No, it is also up to ME and YOU to safeguard these rights too. We have an obligation to act and to make choices that do not harm anyone and to respect the universal code of conduct.

"Shopping" by Jantien Roozenburg, 15, The Netherlands

How is a rug made?
Children in many countries are sold into bonded labor and made to work for a few pennies a week. Many of them make hand-knotted rugs. It matters little to the bosses that the children work many hours a day, or are subjected to stress-related illnesses. In the early 1990's, a coalition of nongovernmental organizations, importers, exporters, and consumer organizations began work that resulted in setting up the RUGMARK Foundation. The Foundation runs a labeling program to certify rugs not made by child labor.

Next time that you or your family buy a rug, look for the mark. Don't take part in this vicious circle of child labor.

Make the right choice

All sorts of goods—soccer balls, cloth and textiles, shoes, coffee—can be produced cheaply through exploitation of workers. Try to find out about the companies who produce the items you buy. Often newspapers and TV news reports expose a company's bad working conditions. Keep your ears and eyes open, and buy goods that give workers a fair deal.

The vegetables on our plates

When growing foods to sell to wealthy countries, a local population may be unable to grow the food that it needs. Ica, Peru, is such a place. Most local farmland is used to grow vegetables for export. In early 1998, Ica's river burst its banks, destroying most of the fields. This meant that there was not enough work for all the people, and the export companies were able to pay them even less than before. The daily wage dropped from 7 soles (a little over $2) to 5 soles—for a 12-hour day in the hot sun! Why should these people suffer to provide us with these items? Who's responsible?

Game of soccer?

66 Soccer has always been one of my favorite sports. I love choosing new balls. One day, I was lucky enough to visit the city of Sialkot, Pakistan. All types of bats, balls, and gloves that are used all over the world are produced here. But the most famous product is the soccer ball!

I visited the leading factory and saw millions of very high-quality balls. Then I came across young children stitching patches of leather. Their hands were filthy and pierced with holes from the needles, and their eyes were red and watering because of the fumes released by the machinery. The whole factory was full of children stitching with all their might. They were aged between 6 and 15. 99

Zulfiqar Ali
Mahar, 14,
Pakistan

"Footballer" by Sanid Zuko, 18, Bosnia-Herzegovina

In all parts of the world, no society, no human being, should take it upon her or himself to act in such a way as to destroy the rights which you have just been reading about.

We all agree that the Declaration is brilliant, BUT we noticed that it can seem to contradict itself if people manipulate an Article to allow them to do exactly the opposite of what another Article intends. For example, you could quote Article 19 as an excuse for making racist remarks. "I'm using my right to free expression!" you claim. But you are also being discriminatory (Article 2) and exercising a right contrary to the spirit of the United Nations (Article 29). If everyone abused Article 22, we would all sit back and rely on others to look after us. And Article 15 would seem to give anyone the right to choose their nationality, requiring the United States, for example, to give U.S. citizenship to anyone who wanted it—something it could never do.

So the Universal Declaration must be read with a little common sense. "Do as you would be done by" is at the heart of it. This is a fragile concept. Many people don't pay any attention to it. It means that we should treat people fairly and honestly, and protect them with a good system of policing and law. Do you think the Universal Declaration should be enforced?

Alexander Solzhenitsyn, a Russian writer, spent eight years in a prison camp after he was falsely accused of a political crime.
66 *The best document the UN put out in all its existence was the Universal Declaration of Human Rights, yet it did not even try to make endorsement of it an obligatory condition of membership. Thus, it left ordinary people at the mercy of governments often not of their choosing.* 99
Alexander Solzhenitsyn, address after receiving the 1970 Nobel Prize for Literature

John Le Carré, an English writer famous for his spy stories, believes in the huge potential of the Universal Declaration.
66 *In the future, I imagine the UN being able to interpose itself between belligerents. I believe there should be a clearly defined limit upon the powers of a national government to inflict misery or hardship on their own citizens, whether this means interceding in Iraq on behalf of the Marsh Arabs and the Kurds, or in Russia on behalf of Muslim minorities.* 99
John Le Carré, 1995

The Universal Declaration is there to protect you—use it, don't abuse it.

Illustration opposite: by
Agne Petiaityte, 12,
Lithuania

We are born into a world in which freedoms and rights
must be both protected and enjoyed.

Great Declaration...
...but what are **we** doing about it?

What you can do

Illustration opposite: submitted by
the Human Rights Education Programme, Pakistan

Who is helping?

Behind closed doors

Some years ago, it was generally felt that what a husband did to his wife or children in the privacy of his own home was his business. In the same way, governments could do what they wanted to their citizens in their own country, and no international organization could poke its nose in and tell them what to do.

This is why we have the Universal Declaration of Human Rights. Throughout the last half of the 1900's, several organizations worked to make these rights real for everyone. Chief among them is the United Nations.

Human rights are at the heart of the UN's activities. The United Nations drafted the Declaration, along with most human rights laws. It is urging governments to respect your rights.

In support of the United Nations, there are several hands reaching out to help those whose rights are abused. The following organizations are among those who are helping to promote human rights.

Commission on Human Rights

This commission, made up of representatives from 53 governments, meets at the UN to consider individual and group complaints about abuses of human rights. It prepares reports and gives instructions for specially appointed people to investigate claims of abuses. As an intergovernmental body, this is the most powerful arm protecting our human rights.

Regional Courts of Human Rights

In Europe, the Americas, and Africa, separate declarations of human rights have been prepared to reflect the historic cultures of the regions. Courts of Human Rights have been set up in Europe and the Americas to hear cases of abuse. Governments often find their own procedures more acceptable than those of distant international bodies. The European Court in particular has made some very dramatic decisions criticizing the British and other governments.

Internati... Crimi... ...urts

You may have heard about the prosecution of war criminals by courts set up to deal ...th the problems in former Yugoslavia ... ...wanda. A permanent International Cri... ...al Court has been scheduled to be ...et up. It will have independent p...secutors who can bring before it any ...rant who is oppressing his or her ...people. No longer will the tyrants ...you have read about go free and ...unpunished.

Committees looking after Conventions

Various Conventions, including the Convention on the Rights of the Child, each have a special Committee set up to look after them. These Committees require governments who have ratified a Convention to report on how well they are complying with it. If you think your government should be doing more, you can write to the United Nations Commission on Human Rights, Palais des Nations, CH-1211, Geneva, Switzerland, and they will investigate.

UN High Commissioner for Human Rights

The Office of the High Commissioner for Human Rights is the body that works to improve human rights laws, to encourage more governments to agree to them, and to promote education about them.

Illustration by Anonymous, Pakistan

Time to **join in...**

...and protect our human rights and the rights of others.

Most people have heard of Amnesty International (see pages 80-81), but there are lots of other groups out there working away on a daily basis to protect the rights of people who are in no position to do so themselves. Here are just a few of the many groups that we know of. Join one of them or find out which other groups are working in your area!

Anti-Slavery International (ASI)

Anti-Slavery International was founded in 1839 and is the world's oldest international human rights organization. ASI campaigns for the freedom of millions of people worldwide who are trapped in situations of slavery or slavery-type practices. It campaigns against exploitation of child labor; commercial sexual exploitation of children, particularly when connected with tourism; abuse of migrant workers who are trapped and exploited by their employers; bonded labor; early and forced marriage of women and children; trafficking of women for sexual exploitation and all forms of forced prostitution; forced labor; the illegal recruitment of workers by governments, political parties, or private individuals, under threat of violence or other penalty; exploitation of indigenous peoples for their labor, land, and other resources.

Contact: The Stableyard, Broomgrove Road,
  London SW9 9TL, UK
email: antislavery@gn.apc.org
Website:www.tcol.co.uk/comorg/assi.htm

Article 12

Article 12 of the Convention on the Rights of the Child (CRC) states that all children capable of making up their minds will have the right to express an opinion on matters that concern them. In the UK, Article 12 is an organization run for young people by young people to ensure that whatever their age, they help decide on what happens in their schools, have a say in local community issues, and are allowed to listen in when plans are being made about their future. These are fundamental rights for children. Article 12 protects them!

Contact: 8 Wakley Street,
  London EC1V 7QE, UK
email: info@article12.uk.com
Website: www.article12.org/

AFAPREDESA

Since the Moroccan occupation of Western Sahara in 1976, many Saharawi people have been imprisoned without trial, tortured, and kept in horrendous conditions. Lots of organizations exist to support them, particularly in Spain. One, called AFAPREDESA, works collecting and publicizing information about violations of human rights. AFAPREDESA also adopts prisoners or those who have "disappeared," and asks the Moroccan government officials about their fate and their whereabouts. Its members also participate in an annual student march to Western Sahara to draw attention to the plight of the territory, and to bring hope to its people by showing that others care!

Contact: Oficina de AFAPREDESA para-España
  José Ortega y Gasset, 77-2 Piso A
  28006 Madrid, Spain
email: afapredesa@derechos.org
Website: www.derechos.org/afapredesa

If you have any problems contacting the organizations on these pages, please get in touch with **Peace Child International** (see page 96).

Amnesty International
See pages 80–81.

Defense for Children International (DCI)

DCI is a children's rights organization founded exclusively to promote and protect the rights of the child. It has grown to become an international network with members in over 70 countries. DCI played a considerable part in the drafting process of the Convention on the Rights of the Child. Today its International Secretariat works closely with many other children's rights organizations to examine whether the Convention is being followed.

Contact: Defense for Children International
    C.P. 618, CH-1212 Grand-Lancy 1
    Geneva, Switzerland
email: dci-hq@pingnet.ch
Website: childhouse.uio.no/childrens_rights/
dci-what.html

Children of the Andes

Children of the Andes is a small British charity dedicated to improving the lives of children at risk in Colombia. It funds projects such as a rehabilitation center for street children and a "flying doctor" service for children in remote rain forests. It supports Fundación Niños de los Andes, which provides a home, schooling, and a future for youngsters who live on the streets of Bogotá. Children and schools are great fund-raisers for this charity. You can help too!

Contact: Unit 4, Enterprise House
    55-59 Upper Ground
    London SE1 9PQ, UK
email: info@children_of_the_andes.org
Website: www.children_of_the_andes.org

Christian Aid

Most aid organizations and religious groups fight for human rights because they know that development and prosperity cannot last where there is no strong culture of human rights. As part of its work, Christian Aid campaigns to change the rules that keep poor people poor. International debt and fair trade are key issues.It was at the forefront of the anti-apartheid movement in the 1980's.

Contact: P.O. Box 100,
    London SE1 7RT, UK
email: info@christian_aid.org
Website: www.christian_aid.org.uk

Free Tibet Campaign

In 1950, China took control of Tibet. The Tibetans were deprived of their nationality and many Buddhist monks and nuns were killed while their temples and treasures were destroyed. Organizations have sprung up around the world to campaign against the action of the Chinese—several of them led by famous film stars such as Richard Gere.

Free Tibet Campaign stands up for the Tibetans' right to decide their own future. It is independent of all governments and is funded by its members and supporters. Its aims are that children may return to Tibet in peace and that the Tibetan people may live as they please and speak their own language. The Tibet House Trust exists to relieve the poverty of Tibetans in exile, to provide educational materials in their language, and to support the exiled government of the Dalai Lama.

Contact: 1 Rosoman Place,
    London EC1R OJY, UK
email: tibetsupport@gn.apc.org
Website: www.freetibet.org

International Save the Children Alliance

The International Save the Children Alliance works in over 100 countries to promote children's rights. Its founder, Eglantyne Jebb (1876–1928), drafted the first-ever statement of the rights of the child. A lot of its work involves raising awareness of children's rights among teachers, social workers, politicians, and journalists, as well as among children and young people themselves. Increasingly, the Alliance is helping to make sure that children's voices are heard on all matters that affect them.

Contact: 59 chemin Moise-Doboule
    1209 Geneva, Switzerland
email: alliance@iprolink.ch
Website: www.savechildren.or.jp/alliance

Illustration by Damien Boltauzer, 13, Canada

Amnesty International

In 1961, a British lawyer named Peter Benenson wrote a newspaper article urging people everywhere to work peacefully for the release of prisoners of conscience, people who have been imprisoned for speaking their minds. The reaction was immediate. Within a month, more than 1,000 people from all over the world had responded. From this grew an organization that has over a million members in more than 160 countries. Amnesty International is now the biggest and most important human rights group in the world! Approximately 400 people work at its International Headquarters in London.

Its members are concerned with all aspects of human rights and use the 30 Articles you've been reading about as the basis for their campaigns. Amnesty International is very independent and has strict principles about accepting donations. A lot of its work is focused on people who have been unfairly imprisoned and those who are being tortured or generally harshly treated.

Amnesty International tries to raise awareness about abuses of human rights because global attention often forces governments into action. It does this in many ways, which include writing letters to prisoners and governments. In many cases, the people who write these letters don't receive replies and never find out whether they got through or not, but their efforts and attention generally do have a positive effect.

If you're going to get angry with authorities, it is vital that you get your facts straight. Amnesty International spends a lot of time ensuring that information is accurate and up to date. The organization is interested in all aspects of children's rights and many of their volunteers are young people. Get involved! To find out more, contact:
AI 322 8th Ave., New York, NY 10001, USA; or
4F, 214 Montreal Rd. Vanier, Ontario, K1L 1A4, Canada.
email: admin-us@aiusa.org or info@amnesty.ca
Website: www.amnesty.org

action from Amnesty International

1 Debates. As you read this book, was there any controversial subject that you felt particularly strongly about? Organize two teams and debate the issue.

2 Exhibitions. Make an exhibition about how things are made and where the products come from. Amnesty cannot provide you with research material on this, but some of the organizations listed on pages 78 and 79 will.

3 A human rights zone. Declare your school, home, or local area a "human rights zone." Make sure that everyone within it respects people's rights and knows what their rights are.

4 Drama. Staging plays is a great way of getting across your message. You could put on plays or sketches about the different articles. But remember to invite important decision-makers so that your ideas will have a positive effect.

5 A human rights mural. Is there a wall in your school or community center that can be decorated with stories of human rights? You may wish to turn it into a history of human rights in your area, so that everyone knows who their local human rights heroes are.

6 International Days. Celebrate the special days throughout the year that commemorate important groups or events. Here are a few dates for your diary: March 8, Women's Day; May 1, International Labor Day; June 5, World Environment Day; July 11, World Population Day; November 20, International Children's Day; December 10, Human Rights' Day; December 15, U.S. Bill of Rights Day.

7 Human-rights awards. Find out who has been doing great work promoting human rights in your area and present them with an award. Invite everyone you know to the award ceremony, including the local press so that they can spread the good news.

8 A human rights fair. Organize speakers to give informative speeches, invite local charities to put up displays, and create posters that tell people about their rights.

9 Letter writing. Get in touch with your local Amnesty International Section and find out how you can help them with their letter-writing campaigns.

10 Videos. Make a video on a specific issue that you are particularly concerned about. Make sure that you try to show both sides of the story. Once you have finished, organize a showing for your friends and family, or contact a local TV station and see if they will air your video.

Global action

Human rights are not something to be defended only by grown-ups at the United Nations or by governments. They are values and principles that every single member of society must believe in and fight for—and that includes YOU!

Free The Children

Twelve year-old Craig Kielburger was deeply touched when he heard that Iqbal Masih, a boy his age, had been murdered after speaking out against a lifetime of slavery (see page 27). When Craig discovered that 250 million children between the ages of 8 and 14 work in slavelike conditions, he knew he had to take action. He told his friends and organized an international campaign to "Free the Children." In the last two years, he has done much to tackle the issue of child labor. He has raised money for education centers and to buy cows and sewing machines so that families still have an income once their children have stopped working.

Craig reads about world developments so that he can never be accused of being naïve.
❝*As young people, we have learned that knowledge is power. Child labor is a very complex issue but that is no excuse to ignore the problem. Who better than children to feel and understand the needs of other children?***❞**

To find out more, contact: FTC, 16 Thornbank Road, Thornhill, Ontario L4J 2A2, Canada
email: freechild@clo.com

The Global March

Imagine former child workers and street children from three continents marching to ask for their right to play, dance, and go to school. In January 1998, the dream came true as the Global March began in the Philippines, South Africa, and Brazil. After marching through their own continents, the three groups met up in Geneva, Switzerland, in June for a Conference on Child Labor. Sophie Scott-Brown reported from Nepal for the BBC:
❝ *For me, a 12-year-old called Marnder symbolized the problem. She worked 16 hours a day chipping stones to look after her huge family. She said, 'I'd like to go to school, but how can I when I have to work?' That summed it up for me! It was a Global March for education, child rights, and equal choices for myself and Marnder.* **❞**

Illustration by Jantien Roozenburg, 15, The Netherlands

"I've joined the march to show my support. Life should be a wonderful experience with children learning in schools and living happily with their parents. But this is not true in much of my country and other places in Africa. Many children have to work very hard because of poverty. This Global March should make things better, but if it doesn't, watch out! I'll be back."

Therese, 19, Senegal

"To be honest, I'm angry. I learned about the Declaration of Human Rights at school and I thought that it was signed by all the countries in the world. So how is it possible that we live in a world where millions and millions of children work in terrible conditions? How has this happened? How can adults be so cruel? I care about this problem, and I'm here to shout with the other marchers to tell people that it's time to stop writing beautiful declarations and start really doing something."

Andres, 14, Nicaragua

FREE THE CHILDREN

Success stories

Reading this book, you might be thinking, "Wow, there are so many terrible things happening around the world, but how can I make a difference?" Well, follow the example of the groups on these pages. We were sent many, many stories about what young people and children have done to fight against the abuse of human rights. Here are just a few of them.

KURM is a Kenyan youth group from Nairobi. It has been campaigning on a range of issues, including forced marriage and homelessness. This photo shows KURM putting on a play entitled "Freedom to choose your wife or husband." They hope this play will make the audience aware of their own personal freedoms.

Deep in the Amazon jungle, a youth-run environmental group called Misión Rescate-Perú organized a series of workshops about the Universal Declaration as part of the preparations for this book. The children had the chance to speak their mind about what human rights meant to them. They drew pictures for each of the Articles and put them on display in an exhibition.

In Pristina, Yugoslavia, groups such as the Kosovo Postpessimists encourage young people to fight for human rights. They direct their activities toward the media in an effort to spread the word about how human rights are violated in Kosovo. They hope their activities make other people aware of what their rights are and what they really mean.

Peace Child Algeria has been very active in promoting human rights. Its members have held meetings with young people in Berber and Arabic to discuss equality and violations of human rights in their country. They also produced a series of poems about the human rights situation in Algeria.

NATURE is an association of 2,000 young people in Afghanistan. They have set up a youth forum to work with disabled and orphaned children. NATURE has also created a youth TV program that highlights the problems facing young people and children in Afghanistan. This photo shows members of NATURE meeting with a UN Special Rapporteur on Human Rights for Afghanistan.

A UNESCO-associated school from Viersen, Germany, took part in the Global March against Child Labor in Bonn. They gathered paintings of feet from 1,500 students, along with messages for their political leaders. A group of handicapped children, who couldn't draw their feet, took photos so that they could show their solidarity with the Global March.

Making great strides...

Most of the students at the George Mitchell School in East London, England, are from families of Asian, African, or Caribbean backgrounds. Some are asylum seekers. In 1995, a 12-year-old Somali refugee, who had been bullied, got into trouble for fighting back in the playground. The school changed what started off as a problem into a positive experience for everyone. His class decided to find out more about refugees and how schools treat them. They met asylum seekers, visited the House of Commons, and made videos. They also wrote a play, which they have performed on various occasions. They named the project WHY? The students have gained self-confidence, knowledge about refugees, and the realization that they have a lot to offer. They have done two additional projects, one on homelessness and one on bullying. The school is buzzing!

Global Kids Inc. works with young people in New York City, encouraging them to become community leaders and responsible citizens. One of its projects focuses on homelessness both in the city and around the world. The group produced the book *Global Kids' Empowerment Book on Homelessness.* For a year they developed relationships with legal advisers, policymakers, and homeless people. They did research, produced two videos, and have given many presentations to help break down stereotypes and make young people more aware of homelessness. If you are concerned about this issue and want to make a change in your community, this is the book for you!

Illustration by Zarin Hasan, Pakistan

... into the future

What will the world be like in 50 years? Will everybody know about the Universal Declaration or will it be forgotten? Will rights be universally respected? Or will torture, slavery, and war still exist?

We all can dream and we all can hope, but hoping and dreaming are never as good as doing something positive. And if we use the Universal Declaration as a guide, we're sure that the world will become a better place.

The nonviolent activist Gandhi once said, **"**Whenever you are in doubt, ... apply the following test. Recall the face of the poorest person and the weakest man whom you may have seen, and ask yourself, if the step you contemplate is going to be of any use to him. Will he gain anything by it? Will it restore him to a control over his own life and destiny?**"**

We think this is a cool philosophy. When you get out of bed, tomorrow and every day for the rest of your life, think about it.

Illustration by Urjana Shrestha, 18, Nepal

The reference section

Illustration opposite: by Sarah Wilson, 17, UK

The **Universal Declaration**

The UN's plain language version of the Articles was presented on the previous pages as a guide. Following is the original text for each Article.

Article 1. All human beings are born free and equal in dignity and rights. They are endowed with reason and conscience and should act towards one another in a spirit of brotherhood.

Article 2. (1) Everyone is entitled to all the rights and freedoms set forth in this Declaration, without distinction of any kind, such as race, color, sex, language, religion, political or other opinion, national or social origin, property, birth or other status. (2) Furthermore, no distinction shall be made on the basis of the political, jurisdictional or international status of the country or territory to which a person belongs, whether it be independent, trust, non-self-governing or under any other limitation of sovereignty.

Article 3. Everyone has the right to life, liberty and security of person.

Article 4. No one shall be held in slavery or servitude; slavery and the slave trade shall be prohibited in all their forms.

Article 5. No one shall be subjected to torture or to cruel, inhuman or degrading treatment or punishment.

Article 6. Everyone has the right to recognition everywhere as a person before the law.

Article 7. All are equal before the law and are entitled without any discrimination to equal protection of the law. All are entitled to equal protection against any discrimination in violation of this Declaration and against any incitement to such discrimination.

Article 8. Everyone has the right to an effective remedy by the competent national tribunals for acts violating the fundamental rights granted him by the constitution or by law.

Article 9. No one shall be subjected to arbitrary arrest, detention or exile.

Article 10. Everyone is entitled in full equality to a fair and public hearing by an independent and impartial tribunal, in the determination of his rights and obligations and of any criminal charge against him.

Article 11. (1) Everyone charged with a penal offense has the right to be presumed innocent until proved guilty according to law in a public trial at which he has had all the guarantees necessary for his defense. (2) No one shall be held guilty of any penal offense on account of any act or omission which did not constitute a penal offense, under national or international law, at the time when it was committed. Nor shall a heavier penalty be imposed than the one that was applicable at the time the penal offense was committed.

Article 12. No one shall be subjected to arbitrary interference with his privacy, family, home or correspondence, nor to attacks upon his honor and reputation. Everyone has the right to the protection of the law against such interference or attacks.

Article 13. (1) Everyone has the right to freedom of movement and residence within the borders of each state. (2) Everyone has the right to leave any country, including his own, and to return to his country.

Article 14. (1) Everyone has the right to seek and to enjoy in other countries asylum from persecution. (2) This right may not be invoked in the case of prosecutions genuinely arising from non-political crimes or from acts contrary to the purposes and principles of the United Nations.

Article 15. (1) Everyone has the right to a nationality. (2) No one shall be arbitrarily deprived of his nationality nor denied the right to change his nationality.

Article 16. (1) Men and women of full age, without any limitation due to race, nationality or religion, have the right to marry and to found a family. They are entitled to equal rights as to marriage, during marriage and at its dissolution. (2) Marriage shall be entered into only with the free and full consent of the intending spouses. (3) The family is the natural and fundamental group unit of society and is entitled to protection by society and the State.

Article 17. (1) Everyone has the right to own property alone as well as in association with others. (2) No one shall be arbitrarily deprived of his property.

Article 18. Everyone has the right to freedom of thought, conscience and religion; this right includes freedom to change his religion or belief, and freedom, either alone or in community with others and in public or private, to manifest his religion or belief in teaching, practice, worship and observance.

# of Human Rights

Article 19. Everyone has the right to freedom of opinion and expression; this right includes freedom to hold opinions without interference and to seek, receive and impart information and ideas through any media and regardless of frontiers.

Article 20. (1) Everyone has the right to freedom of peaceful assembly and association. (2) No one may be compelled to belong to any association.

Article 21. (1) Everyone has the right to take part in the government of his country, directly or through freely chosen representatives. (2) Everyone has the right of equal access to public service in his country. (3) The will of the people shall be the basis of the authority of government; this will shall be expressed in periodic and genuine elections which shall be by universal and equal suffrage and shall be held by secret vote or by equivalent free voting procedures.

Article 22. Everyone, as a member of a society, has the right to social security and is entitled to realization, through national effort and international co-operation and in accordance with the organization and resources of each State, of the economic, social and cultural rights indispensable for his dignity and the free development of his personality.

Article 23. (1) Everyone has the right to work, to free choice of employment, to just and favorable conditions of work and to protection against unemployment. (2) Everyone, without any discrimination, has the right to equal pay for equal work. (3) Everyone who works has the right to just and favorable remuneration ensuring for himself and his family an existence worthy of human dignity, and supplemented, if necessary, by other means of social protection. (4) Everyone has the right to form and to join trade unions for the protection of his interests.

Article 24. Everyone has the right to rest and leisure, including reasonable limitation of working hours and periodic holidays with pay.

Article 25. (1) Everyone has the right to a standard of living adequate for the health and well-being of himself and his family, including food, clothing, housing and medical care and necessary social services, and the right to security in the event of unemployment, sickness, disability, widowhood, old age or other lack of livelihood in circumstances beyond his control. (2) Motherhood and childhood are entitled to special care and assistance. All children, whether born in or out of wedlock, shall enjoy the same social protection.

Article 26. (1) Everyone has the right to education. Education shall be free, at least in the elementary and fundamental stages. Elementary education shall be compulsory. Technical and professional education shall be made generally available and higher education shall be equally accessible to all on the basis of merit. (2) Education shall be directed to the full development of the human personality and to the strengthening of respect for human rights and fundamental freedoms. It shall promote understanding, tolerance and friendship among all nations, racial or religious groups, and shall further the activities of the United Nations for the maintenance of peace. (3) Parents have a prior right to choose the kind of education that shall be given to their children.

Article 27. (1) Everyone has the right freely to participate in the cultural life of the community, to enjoy the arts and to share in scientific advancement and its benefits. (2) Everyone has the right to the protection of the moral and material interests resulting from any scientific, literary or artistic production of which he is the author.

Article 28. Everyone is entitled to a social and international order in which the rights and freedoms set forth in this Declaration can be fully realized.

Article 29. (1) Everyone has duties to the community in which alone the free and full development of his personality is possible. (2) In the exercise of his rights and freedoms, everyone shall be subject only to such limitations as are determined by law solely for the purpose of securing due recognition and respect for the rights and freedoms of others and of meeting the just requirements of morality, public order and the general welfare in a democratic society. (3) These rights and freedoms may in no case be exercised contrary to the purposes and principles of the United Nations.

Article 30. Nothing in this Declaration may be interpreted as implying for any State, group or person any right to engage in any activity or to perform any act aimed at the destruction of any of the rights and freedoms set forth herein.

The Convention on

The Convention on the Rights of the Child was adopted by the United Nations General Assembly November 20, 1989. Here is a plain language version from The Save The Children Fund and UNICEF.

Article 1: The Convention defines a child as a person under 18 unless national law recognizes that the age of majority is reached earlier.

Article 2: All the rights laid down in the Convention are to be enjoyed by children regardless of race, color, sex, language, religion, political, or other opinion, national, ethnic, or social origin, property, disability, birth, or other status.

Article 3: All sections concerning the child should be in her/his best interests.

Article 4: The State's obligation to translate the rights of the Convention into reality.

Article 5: The State should respect the rights and responsibilities of parents to provide guidance appropriate to the child's capacities.

Article 6: The right to life.

Article 7: The right to a name and a nationality and, as far as possible, the right to know and to be cared for by her/his parents.

Article 8: The right to protection of her/his identity by the State.

Article 9: The right to live with her/his parents unless incompatible with her/his best interests. The right, if desired, to maintain personal relations and direct contact with both parents if separated from one or both.

Article 10: The right to leave and enter her/his own country, and other countries, for purposes of reunion with parents and maintaining the child-parent relationship.

Article 11: The right to protection by the State if unlawfully taken or kept abroad by a parent.

Article 12: The right to freely express an opinion in all matters affecting her/him and to have that opinion taken into account.

Article 13: The right to express views, and obtain and transmit ideas and information regardless of frontiers.

Article 14: The right to freedom of thought, conscience, and religion, subject to appropriate parental guidance.

Article 15: The right to meet together with other children and join and form associations.

Article 16: The right to protection from arbitrary and unlawful interference with privacy, family, home, and correspondence, and from libel and slander.

Article 17: The right of access to information and materials from a diversity of sources and of protection from harmful materials.

Article 18: The right to benefit from child-rearing assistance and child-care services and facilities provided to parents/guardians by the State.

Article 19: The right to protection from maltreatment by parents or others responsible for her/his care.

Article 20: The right to special protection if s/he is temporarily or permanently deprived of her/his family environment, due regard being paid to her/his cultural background.

Article 21: The right, in countries where adoption is allowed, to have it ensured that an adoption is carried out in her/his best interests.

Article 22: The right, if a refugee, to special protection.

the **Rights of the Child**

Article 23: The right, if disabled, to special care, education, and training to help her/him enjoy a full life in conditions that ensure dignity and promote self-reliance and a full and active life in society.

Article 24: The right to the highest standard of health and medical care attainable.

Article 25: The right, if placed by the State for purposes of care, protection, or treatment, to have all aspects of that placement regularly evaluated.

Article 26: The right to benefit from social security.

Article 27: The right to a standard of living adequate for her/his physical, mental, spiritual, moral, and social development.

Article 28: The right to education, including free primary education. Discipline to be consistent with a child's human dignity.

Article 29: The right to an education that prepares her/him for an active, responsible life as an adult in a free society which respects others and the environment.

Article 30: The right, if a member of a minority community or indigenous people, to enjoy her/his own culture, to practice her/his own religion, and to use her/his own language.

Article 31: The right to rest and leisure, to engage in play, and to participate in recreational, cultural, and artistic activities.

Article 32: The right to protection from economic exploitation and work that is hazardous, interferes with her/his education, or harms her/his health or physical, mental, spiritual, moral, and social development.

Article 33: The right to protection from narcotic drugs and from being involved in their production or distribution.

Article 34: The right to protection from sexual exploitation and abuse.

Article 35: The right to protection from being abducted, sold, or trafficked.

Article 36: The right to protection from all other forms of exploitation.

Article 37: The right not to be subjected to torture or degrading treatment. If detained, not to be kept with adults, sentenced to death, nor imprisoned for life without the possibility of release. The right to legal assistance and contact with family.

Article 38: The right, if below 15 years of age, not to be recruited into armed forces nor to engage in direct hostilities.

Article 39: The right, if the victim of armed conflict, torture, neglect, maltreatment, or exploitation, to receive appropriate treatment for her/his physical and psychological recovery and reintegration into society.

Article 40: The right, if accused or guilty of committing an offense, to age-appropriate treatment likely to promote her/his sense of dignity and worth and her/his reintegration as a constructive member of society.

Article 42: The right to be informed of these principles and provisions by the state in which s/he lives.

Note: The Convention has 54 Articles in all. Articles 41 and 43 to 54 are concerned with its implementation and entry into force.

Glossary

abolition Getting rid of customs, laws, and rules.

Aborigines People who have lived in a place from the earliest known period.

abortion The process of ending a pregnancy.

amnesty A general pardon for people who have been accused of an offense.

apartheid The system that the South African government used for keeping apart people of different races.

arbitrary Depending on someone's personal idea or prejudice.

asylum A safe place where people can go.

autonomy The right for a group of people to govern themselves.

Berlin Wall The barrier that used to separate East and West Germany.

bias A prejudice against something.

bonded labor Where a child is "sold" to an employer in exchange for a loan of money to the family.

boycott Decision by a group of people, governments, or organizations to refuse to deal with a particular person or group.

caste A division of society based on differences of wealth, privileges, or occupation.

child labor Where children have to work to earn a living.

citizenship A person's status as a citizen.

civil rights The personal rights of an individual.

civil war War between different groups of people in the same country.

colonialism Where one country takes control of another country or region.

communism A classless society where the State or the community, not individuals, owns property, factories, and so on.

conscience A person's sense of what is right and what is wrong.

Convention on the Rights of the Child A UN document setting out the rights that all children should have.

copyright Owning an original work, such as a poem, play, or piece of music, and controlling who has the right to use it.

coup Sometimes known as a "coup d'état," where a government is suddenly and often violently taken over by a group of people.

criminal Someone who has broken the law.

culture Beliefs, values, and customs passed down through generations.

death penalty Where people are punished by being put to death.

democracy Government by the people.

developing countries Countries that are trying to build up their industries and the goods they produce.

dictator A ruler who runs a country without allowing any opposition.

disability The loss of some of a person's senses or bodily functions, such as the ability to walk, see or hear.

discrimination Unfair treatment of a person or a certain type of people.

divine right Where a monarch could do as he or she pleased without taking notice of anyone else.

dowry The system whereby a girl's family has to give money or property to the bridegroom when she marries.

eco-friendly Something that doesn't harm the environment.

economic Concerning money and finance.

election The act of voting for somebody to represent you.

empire A whole group of countries and people controlled by one country or ruler.

exile A period of time during which a person is forced to live outside his/her country.

gender Describes whether a person is male or female.

genocide The killing of a whole group or race of people.

Gypsy A cultural group originally from North West India, who are now found all over the world. They like to travel rather than settle in one place.

illiterate Unable to read or write.

independence Freedom from control. When countries get their independence, they are no longer ruled by an outside power.

indigenous Original to a region or country.

Inquisition An effort by the Catholic Church to seek out and punish people who opposed their teachings. The most famous was the Spanish Inquisition.

Koran The sacred book of Islam.

law A rule of conduct laid down by a controlling authority.

legal process Enforcing law or having a remedy at law.

liberty Freedom from control or constraint.

Magna Carta A defining law which stated that a king must rule justly when dealing with his subjects.

massacre Murdering hundreds or even thousands of people at one time.

media A collective term for television, radio, cinema, and press.

nation A group of people united by a common language, history, culture, or government.

nationality A person's legal status as a member of a certain country.

persecute To treat someone badly, usually because of their race, religion, or political beliefs.

principle A standard or rule of conduct.

prohibited Stopped from doing something.

prostitution The performance of sexual acts for payment.

race A group of people who are considered to have the same roots.

rapporteur Someone who prepares a report of a meeting for a higher body.

referendum A vote taken by the people on a certain issue.

refugee A person who has been forced to flee his or her country.

religion An organized system of beliefs, ceremonies, and worship.

Index

revolution A means of radical change that may or may not be violent.

secular Not concerned with religion.

segregate To separate one group of people from another.

skinhead Youths with shaven heads who are often racist.

social security Financial aid given by the State to reduce poverty.

social services The provision by the State of care for the needy.

society The way in which organized groups of people live together.

suttee An extinct custom whereby an Indian widow would be burned alive on her husband's funeral pyre.

Taliban A political and military force that controls most of Afghanistan.

trade union An organization formed to look after the rights of working people.

treaty A formal agreement between two or more governments.

tribe A group of people linked by social or cultural ties.

unemployed Unable to find or do work.

unemployment benefit Money provided by the State to support those out of work.

United Nations (UN) An organization that tries to achieve world peace and foster international co-operation.

Universal Declaration of Human Rights
Refer to pages 8 and 90–91.

values Certain beliefs of what is right and what is wrong.

violation The infringement or denial of a person's rights.

vote A means by which to indicate a choice.

World Health Organization (WHO) A United Nations organization to improve health.

Peace Child International

In Papua New Guinea when warring tribes of headhunters made peace, they gave each other a baby. The children grew up with their new tribes, and if, in the future, conflict threatened, the tribes would send these children to resolve it. Such a child was called a "Peace Child."

Peace Child International was founded in 1982 to give young people the chance to speak out on issues that are important to them. For the first eight years, the main focus was a musical called "Peace Child." It told how young people of warring nations worked together to build peace between their countries through pioneering youth exchanges.

Since 1982, there have been over 5,000 performances of "Peace Child" in over 30 countries. Each performance has been unique in reflecting different youth concerns on global issues. One of the chief concerns has been about environmental issues. Peace Child International moved into publishing to allow young people to express their concerns on paper. Since 1992, three different environmental publications have been written, illustrated, designed, and edited by young people. The most successful to date has been *Rescue Mission Planet Earth—a young people's edition of Agenda 21.* This book was about the plan for the future agreed upon at the Earth Summit in Rio de Janeiro. It was created in the same way as this book and has sold hundreds of thousands of copies in 18 different languages.

Peace Child has close links with the United Nations and works with 500 groups around the world. But what makes it a really unique organization is that young people have a huge role in running it and making decisions about its strategies and projects. The headquarters are in England, where young people from all over the world come and manage projects. They all live in a hostel designed and built by a 19-year-old Czech student. At Peace Child, we are always open to new ideas and searching for new contacts. We have a quarterly newsletter that is written by young people and is distributed worldwide. If you have enjoyed this book and would like to be involved, get in touch. Here are the details:

Peace Child International
The White House, Buntingford,
Herts SG9 9AH, UK
Tel: 44 (0) 1763 274459
Fax: 44 (0) 1763 274460
email: RescueMission@compuserve.com
Website: www.oneworld.org/peacechild

Peace Child International is a British
Registered Charity – No. 284731